Praise for
It's OK to be Spiritual AND Wealthy

"WOW! What a great book! If you're ready to grow personally, professionally and financially, then read and absorb the strategies in this brilliant book by my friend Deborah 'Atianne' Wilson!"

> James Malinchak
> Featured on ABC's Hit TV Show, *Secret Millionaire*
> Founder, www.BigMoneySpeaker.com

"This is a warm, wonderful and uplifting book, full of spiritual guidance and wisdom that shows you how to fulfill your potential and realize the greatness that is within you."

> Brian Tracy
> President, Brian Tracy International

"After reading *It's OK to be Spiritual AND Wealthy*, I am affirmed in what's possible for all of us in this lifetime. While Deborah doesn't actually use the words *Law of Attraction*, this concept is what she's talking about in many of the awesome teachings and applications she offers. She'll teach you how to manifest joy, abundance and prosperity in any area of your life, and equip you with new ways of understanding and implementing manifestation. Don't wait to read this book.

> Patty Aubery
> President, The Canfield Training Group

"I like knowing that Deborah and her book *It's OK to be Spiritual AND Wealthy* are around. As Deborah once said in an interview with me, 'Money is love,' and this lovely book will help so many people realize that abundance and prosperity can be positive forces in our lives. Deborah teaches that not only do you get to create abundance and prosperity in your life, but the Universe also wants you to create more. Imagine that!"

> Kristi Frank
> As seen on *The Apprentice* and *Oprah*
> CEO of KristiFrank.com

"Deborah shares her perspective about the nature of reality and consciously blends the invisible world with the visible seamlessly in *It's Ok to be Spiritual AND Wealthy*. Deborah makes a great argument for our collective purpose being the experiencing and expressing of our divinity in an obviously vast and abundant universe. Each chapter addresses one aspect of flawed thinking and gives exercises for aligning our thoughts with our greatest potential. This is a book to keep and refer to over and over in order to get unstuck from thinking that does not serve our soul's evolution."

Gary Mantz and Suzanne Mitchell
Mantz and Mitchell Radio Show

"*It's OK to be Spiritual AND Wealthy* is such a valuable resource for practical spiritual wisdom. I love how Deborah defines wealth as not just a monetary value but a barometer for joy and satisfaction in all main life areas, such as your health, relationships and spirituality. The steps she offers are manageable and will allow you to see and create shifts where you most need to get unstuck."

Vicki Irvin
CEO, Superwoman Lifestyle
www.VickiIrvin.com

"Deborah is that rare combination of a teacher who has not only extraordinary range and depth but also playfulness and accessibility that is hard to find. She has an amazing ability to take real-life challenges of wealth creation, manifesting, and spiritual practice seem simple and doable for the average person. This book takes the seemingly daunting journey of prosperity and abundance and breaks it down into small, bite-sized steps. This book is for you if you are committed to your own version of wild success and are looking for the perfect partnership of the human and spiritual realm."

Beth Hanishewski
Coach. Speaker. Spiritual Gangster.
www.mindsetcoaching.com

It's OK to be Spiritual AND Wealthy

Heather ~

777 "You have hit the jackpot" of life - there is a clear path you are illuminated and so is your path. All you need to know is the next step. through the trust of your inner voice & loving heart! XO Arianne

Also by Deborah "Atianne" Wilson

Book
Jump-Start Your Success:
23 Top Speakers Share Their Insights for
Creating More Success, Wealth and Happiness

Music
Oneness Becomes You™
"Magnum Opus"
Channeled Music for Your Ascension
~ 11:11 ~
(2-CD set)

Home Study
Trust Your Heart
3 Easy Keys to Unlocking the Power of Your Intuition
and Creating a Spiritual and Wealthy Life
(4-CD set, action guide & journal,
4-CD set transcription)

It's OK to be Spiritual AND Wealthy

19 Essential Keys for Living a Joyful, Prosperous & Abundant Life

Deborah "Atianne" Wilson

WHITE HERON PUBLISHING
Boulder, Colorado

Book design: Deborah "Atianne" Wilson, Erika M. Schreck
Editing: Erika M. Schreck, www.erikaschreck.com
Proofreading: Erika M. Schreck, Dianna Mednick, Suzanne Mitchell
Interview transcription: Cindy McLane, www.transcribeyourbook.com
Cover design: Kendra Dixson, www.kendraart.com

Deborah "Atianne" Wilson is not a medical doctor. This book is not intended as a substitute for the medical advice or treatment from a physician. The reader should regularly consult a physician in matters relating to his/her health and particularly with respect to any symptoms that may require diagnosis or medical attention. The intent of the author is only to offer information of a general nature to help the reader in his/her quest for holistic well-being. In the event the reader uses any of the information in this book, which is his/her constitutional and individual right, the author and the publisher assume no responsibility for the reader's actions or results.

Printed in the USA

Library of Congress Cataloging-in-Publication Data
Wilson, Deborah "Atianne"
  It's OK to be spiritual and wealthy: 19 essential keys for living a joyful,
  prosperous & abundant life / Deborah "Atianne" Wilson
        p. cm.
1. Self-Help. 2. Spirituality. 3. Body, Mind, Spirit.

ISBN-13: 978-0615962931
ISBN-10: 0615962939

WHITE HERON PUBLISHING
Boulder, Colorado

www.whiteheronpublishing.com

Dedicated to Bryce and Katharine

*for gifting me the miracle of giving birth and
all that comes with the path of motherhood*

Contents

I AM

Spiritual AND Wealthy Interviews

Acknowledgments

From the broadest perspective I am truly thankful for *it all*. Every nuance within my life, every experience, every encounter, and everything I once considered to be heartache. All of my life experiences have always been and will continue to be an invitation from Love to Love.

I was naively mistaken when I thought writing a book would be a solitary experience. I am so extraordinarily grateful for the team of "handlers" that kept me moving forward, fed, watered, organized, straightened up/out, laughing, inspired, edited, on track and on purpose.

The manifestation of this book is possible in particular because of some of the most giving people I know who gave their time, their talents and their love to me and this work.

I AM Grateful to...

Erika Schreck, for the gift of your editing expertise and willingness to trust your intuitive voice to interpret and reorganize mine, and for being one of the most loving people I know. Your love, friendship, cheerleading, and commitment to this book encouraged me in ways words are inadequate to express.... *although I am sure I would add "ness" to any of them.*

Beth Hanishewski, for crossing a ballroom to blossom an enduring friendship, snapping me out of it with "What if the book is finished?" and by adding your love to this book and to me by sharing your story, wisdom and expertise in the interview.

Suzanne Mitchell, your thoughts, suggestions and corrections invited me to be even more on target with my thoughts and writing. You easily could see the essence of what wanted to come through and tenderly demanded it to reveal itself through me.

Kendra Dixson, for your willingness to co-create and be playful capturing the essence of the book's inner qualities and artfully expressing them on the cover.

My Beloved Edmund, for finding me *again,* reminding me how *it's supposed to be,* being *all in,* folding things I didn't know were possible to fold, and seeing me through the eyes of the Divine. Your love and dedication to me, my family and my work nourish my soul. *Te amo.*

Dianna Mednick, my mother and soul sister, for imprinting within me the ability to connect with any energy, supporting my family and the menagerie through contrasting times, light balls, foot rubs, aluminum hats, laughing till we cry, showing me that there is beauty in everything, and loving me no matter what. *I love you.*

The Realm of the Unseen, especially the energy of love I recognize as Angels, tears stream down my cheeks as my love for you radiates from my heart with humble gratitude for saving my life by reminding me what was possible and propelling me forward with Unconditional Love.

I Believe

I Believe...

My journey to the awareness that I AM ONE with All That Is has felt both challenging and extraordinary. Everything that I judged as challenging was steeped in human drama and the misunderstanding that I was alone and lacked any control to sustain happiness in my life. Within this illusion and when I most felt alone, I would say to myself that I wanted to *go home*. There was some inner knowing, some deep awareness, that there was this *home*, and, if I could get there, I would feel the peace and happiness that I longed for.

During the times I felt the most despair, I longed to merge with the calm ocean waters near my home. I wanted to leave the planet.

Thankfully, I also had a deep inner knowing that I had made a commitment to my children to stay with them and to be the best me that I could be. The love I have for them and the love I experienced from them became my inspiration to do whatever it would take to be better, to get better and to feel better. What I ultimately realized was that in order to do just that, I needed to love *me*.

As I began to learn to love myself through many wonderful and extremely uncomfortable therapeutic experiences, as well as spiritual books and quiet reflective times, I began to understand that the journey to what I called *home* was something I needed to do while still staying here on the planet in my physical body.

I needed to declare what I call a "Sacred Yes"
and opt back into this life.

As I continued to say *yes* to life, life became more joyful than not.

The scale began to tip, and I began to have more extraordinary experiences than challenging ones. I also learned how to move more quickly than I had previously through the stuff I felt was challenging.

The extraordinary experiences I have had and continue to have are sometimes difficult for me to articulate. I remember when I first became aware and started to share that I could see energy, and a dear friend of mine asked me if I thought I might have a brain tumor. By this point in my journey, I clearly knew I did not have tumor! I also knew that what was happening in, around and through me was not only completely normal for me to experience but is also possible for each of us.

Extraordinary experiences have now become more my norm. Every step of the way, as I said *yes* to life, I began to feel more love, more courage, more faith and more trust in myself and in the world around me.

For me, *going home* was discovering that we are all an extension of Unconditional Love. Through my stillest moments and through the darkest nights of my soul's experience, my tears of desperation have been replaced with tears of pure joy, as I remember that there is more to this physical life experience than meets the eye.

As we allow ourselves to heal any ideas of separation, we begin to discover our true worth, our true magnificence and our true creative power as Divine beings. It is up to each of us to allow ourselves quiet time to revel in our own reflection through the loving eyes of All That Is.

Some of what I have come to believe from my inner journey and outer experience is highlighted in this book. May what I have discovered for myself inspire you to consciously connect with whatever you call your Higher Power, so you will discover the answers that are perfect for your soul's journey.

What I Believe, as well as the entirety of this book, is offered to support you with Love.

To your Spiritual AND Wealthy Journey,

Deborah "Atianne" Wilson

What I Believe...

I believe we are all miracles.

I believe we are Beings of Light here to uncover, discover and play in the energy of the infinite possibilities and experiences that have never been done, experienced or brought forth into this plane of existence ever before.

I believe that each one of us is good and worthy and that there is nothing wrong with us—with the exception of what we *think* is wrong with us.

I believe we chose in.

I believe we were chosen.

I believe while we experience this human form, we are at choice to choose again.

I believe any struggle and suffering that is experienced is simply not choosing the true reality of who and what we really are.

I believe we are Holy beings.

I believe we all came to find our way back to a place of deep awareness of our collective connection.

I believe this is our awakening.

I believe that in our awakening and further revealing of the truth of ourselves, we remember the vibration of creation, joy, love, forgiveness, health and wealth.

I believe we knew that we were always on a mission to find our way home.

I believe we knew before we came that this earthly experience was an illusion.

I believe we thought it would be easy and fun and an adventure.

I believe our soul still sees it this way and the dark to overcome is merely the *egoic* force that is ultimately our gift, in that it is our greatest opponent.

I believe the *egoic* nature has been perfectly placed for each of us to meet and subsequently overcome in our remembering who we are and what we are capable of.

I believe that it is in knowing the Self, in the remembering, in being true to the Self and in trusting the Divine connection that we can live fully in our purpose and passions, providing even more expansion of light to ourselves, our brothers and sisters, and even other dimensions, all encompassed by the ONE.

You are Loved.

We Are Always Creating

It is your Divine birthright to create anything you want in your earthly life. You are the outer-most directive expression of Co-Creative Energy. YOU are here to play and grow and expand that energy.

You get to play out this life,
your **life, any way you want.**

Even as a little girl, I knew that if I wanted something, I could make it happen. Children are very clear about their ability to co-create and manifest their ideas and desires into reality. Each of us did this with ease and grace until someone told us we couldn't. Then, for some of us, life got a bit bumpy as we took on other people's beliefs, rather than believing in ourselves and our own abilities.

Just for a moment, remember a time when you really wanted something to happen, and you were able to bring it into your life. You were clear about what you wanted, you thought about it a lot, and you imagined what it was like to have it. In other words, you were already experiencing it in the NOW. The feelings associated with this experience were good feelings, bringing you a sense of joy and well-being.

Now, remember a time when you worried about something happening that you didn't want, and it happened anyway. Just like the "positive" experience, you were clear about what you didn't want, you thought about it a lot, and you imagined what it would be like if it were to happen. In other words, you were experiencing it in the NOW, and your thoughts created anxious feelings, which brought a sense of fear and anxiety.

Both of these scenarios exist because this field of Co-Creative Energy is operating *every* second of *every* minute of *every* hour of *every* day of *every* week of *every* month of *every* year, and this Energy never *ever* takes a break or a holiday. You are receiving *exactly* what you are extending energetically.

Whether you are aware of or believe in this Co-Creative Energy, it's doing its thing. However, when you are aware, and when you allow yourself to become playful with this knowing and your own power to create, then you can become the conscious, joyful co-creator of your own destiny.

Ask, Listen and Take Guided Action

One of my very favorite quotes comes from Michael Bernard Beckwith who said, "You can't hide your secret thoughts because they show up as your life." These thoughts are both conscious and subconscious beliefs that are directing your life. Both can be changed in any direction that you desire.

In my life, positive change happens when I take action based on my intuitive guidance. First, I ask what I call *clarifying questions*. Then, I *listen* for the answers and take what I call *guided action*. I trust that my questions are always answered, and it is up to me to be unattached to what the answer is or how it shows up.

What I love about honoring my intuition and the spirit world is that I get what I call *insider information*. At any moment I can access wisdom and information that allow me to be happier, healthier and wealthier in my personal life, while also using this insider information to guide, inspire and show others how to do the same.

One morning I was thinking about how so many beliefs about money, spirituality and relationships keep people stuck in a vicious cycle of victimization. So, I asked the angelic realm what I needed to know about these limiting beliefs. True to angelic form, they offered a perspective and definition larger than I expected:

**True Spiritual Wealth comes from knowing
that your thoughts create your reality.**

Spiritual AND Wealthy people understand this truth and are mindful of what they say, how they feel and what they do. They understand that how they spend their time and with whom makes a difference in the life that they are co-creating.

This information and initial awareness can be a bit shocking for most people at first. It takes courage to reconcile that ultimately each and every one of us is responsible for the choices we make in our thoughts, feelings and actions.

Once we awaken to this awareness, we can then consciously focus our Co-Creative Energy in amazing and thrilling ways that often seem magical. More importantly, we can create a life we love.

My Own Powerful Transformation

At one point in my life, I was extremely ill. Within a seven-year period, I was diagnosed with and treated for cancer and then an autoimmune disorder that turned out to be far more physically and emotionally life-changing than the cancer had ever been. My doctor told me that there was no cure and that the painful, debilitating and life-altering level of dis-ease that I was experiencing would stay the same or get worse.

During one of my most miserable days experiencing this dis-ease, I lay in bed, freezing. I was unable to sustain a normal body temperature, even though I was fully clothed and covered with multiple blankets and a heating pad. Ironically, this day would become one of my most life-defining days and moments.

I remember quietly saying, "This house is so cold."

Instantly, I heard a voice so clearly and beautifully say, "You need to leave this house."

I AM

I asked, "Why?"

I then heard, "Because there is a better life waiting for you."

I asked, "When?"

I then heard, "Less than two years."

And that was it. The conversation ended.

The room continued to hold a palpable presence and familiar stillness, which was infused with the comfort of hope and love—and a sense of normalcy. I felt profound clarity, and I felt safe.

As I wondered about the words spoken, "There's a better life waiting for you," I imagined that if a better life was waiting for me, *then it had to be better than what I was currently experiencing.*

Then, intuitively I knew that if my body "could get into this mess," then my body "could also get out of this mess." I was clear that if I expected my health and my life at that time to be different, it was going to be up to me to make it happen. That knowledge and awareness of personal responsibility changed my life forever.

Within the next two years, I shifted my diet, did transformational work, moved my family out of state, ended a 23-year-old relationship and changed careers. *My positive changes required more than just thinking positively*; they required my asking Spirit for help, listening to the guidance given, and taking action that sometimes felt uncomfortable and terrifying. I healed my body, and the positive shifts rippled throughout every area of my life.

**When you change your attitude and actions, you
can quickly create a positive impact on your life.
In fact, when each of us positively changes our
own life, we also positively affect those around us.**

When we consciously connect to Spirit, we experience a dramatic increase in synchronistic events or what many people call *coincidences*.

I personally don't believe in coincidences because they imply randomness without cause and effect, which is in complete contrast to what was given to me by the very definition of "True Spiritual Wealth," the essence of Spiritual Law.

Everything that makes itself known in your life is perfectly aligned and matches your Co-Creative Energy. What we think and feel about what shows up gifts us a great opportunity to get curious and notice whether we are happy with our results. If we are not happy with the results in our life, we can choose differently, creating *new agreements* with ourselves and others.

Your life can then become what it was truly meant to be, an expression of what you want and desire as a direct result of your conscious Co-Creative Energy.

Co-Creative Energy Has Many Names

Each religion and group of individuals that allow a space for what they believe to be sacred have a name for this energy. "IT" has been called the Universe, Divine, Source, God, Oneness, Quantum Field, Unconditional Love, Infinity and so on. So far, I've referenced "IT" in several ways and will continue to do so in this book as a way of supporting the collective healing and understanding that there are specific words that call each of us to awaken. While one person may resonate with *God*, another may resonate with *Source*.

Deep healing occurs when we realize that vibrationally there is no "wrong" word for this Co-Creative Energy. Any word that awakens *your* inner knowing can only be "right."

So, it doesn't matter what you call "IT." From the angelic perspective, "it matters not what you call us, just that you do." We can label "IT" in many creative ways, yet it does not change the truth: "IT" just is and always will be.

Let's consider gravity. You can call it by any name, you can believe in its existence or not, yet the truth remains the same: it just is. Having awareness and an appreciation of the Law of Gravity, for example, can and does have a direct effect on your life. Gravity, just like Co-Creative Energy, is doing its thing, despite our beliefs about it or what we call it or how we name it.

Open to Your True Spiritual Wealth

The more you open your awareness to your "True Spiritual Wealth," the wealthier you become, not only from a spiritual standpoint but also from a material one:

**True Material Wealth comes from
feeling joyful about what you created.**

From this angelic perspective, we are invited to open up and go beyond our current collective and individual beliefs about what "Material Wealth" really means. Like anything in our lives, the meaning, value and beliefs we place on something deem it "positive" or "negative."

"Material" then becomes everything that you have and experience in your life, which has come into form from your consistent thoughts and feelings. Regardless of *what you have, how you feel about what you have* becomes the true mechanism for measuring your Material Wealth.

The essence of True Material Wealth is not saying that you should feel joyful about something like cancer. Rather, as we evaluate our emotional state, based on this definition, we have an opportunity to change the direction of our lives when we realize that what we have created is not feeling joyful to us and that we can make new choices.

I was not happy about having cancer, nor was I joyful about the prognosis or effects of the autoimmune dis-ease. However, I realized that I could choose to get very curious about my life and take responsibility for how it was playing out at that time.

I actually was so irritated at the doctor and his bleak opinion of how things were going to go for me that I got clear very quickly that I was going to prove him wrong. Anger became a positive aspect of my initial motivation, and getting well became a place of determination and excitement. It turned out he was the perfect doctor for me and for my healing because he guided me in a synchronistic way to heal myself.

I got curious and asked Spirit to show me how I was going to return to health. Then, I paid attention to everything and everyone that even hinted at being answers to my question. As I paid attention to the ideas and inspirations that I attracted, I took action. I expected to heal, saw myself healed, and felt what it would be like to return to health.

If you're not experiencing joy, direct *only* positive thoughts and feelings toward any outcome you desire. As you learn to create more experiences that feel joyful, and focus more of your attention on joy and *feeling* joy, you will increase your ability to attract and manifest more joyful outcomes. Starting where you are right now, you can easily evaluate from the angelic perspective how Spiritual AND Wealthy you are.

It doesn't matter what you have; it only matters how you *feel* about what you have.

"It's OK to be Spiritual AND Wealthy"

Perhaps you have picked up this book because you want something to be different in your life and you believe an increase in your level of financial flow is one of your answers. Or, maybe you're attracted to this book because you feel relatively comfortable in *making money*, but you feel some stirring or calling within you that there is *something more*.

The idea of this book was born out of a conversation about how passionate I am about dispelling the false ideas that we must choose spirituality over wealth or wealth over spirituality.

Regardless of what you have learned and what you currently believe, you don't need to choose between being spiritual *or* wealthy because these concepts are not mutually exclusive.

All misunderstandings about what constitutes being a spiritual person, a wealthy person, or a Spiritual AND Wealthy person have been steeped in generations of *egoic* thinking, teaching and behavior.

Phrases like "money is the root of all evil" perpetuate the mindset that money is bad; so, if you want to create significant financial abundance, you may be judged as being evil, shallow or materialistic—and certainly not spiritual.

The same misaligned thinking condemns "spiritual people" as being greedy and untrustworthy if they choose to teach anything deemed religious or spiritual while *earning a living* or creating extraordinary income from doing what they love. Why would you want to create more income if you are surrounded by family, friends or a community that may judge you as being evil, shallow, greedy or untrustworthy?

People have a variety of beliefs about how they define and understand *spiritual* and *wealthy*. We sabotage delicious possibilities in multiple areas of our lives when we don't investigate the validity of our beliefs or challenge ourselves to shift our mindset when we discover anything incongruent between our limited beliefs and our heart's desires.

Without constant conscious awareness and a strong spiritual practice, the views and beliefs of the collective consciousness can affect your beliefs, choices and life experiences.

Because most individuals keep *spiritual* and *wealthy* separate, they don't believe that *It's OK to be Spiritual AND Wealthy.*

You create lack and limitation within some part of your life when you have any negative thoughts about spirituality, wealth or the ability to *be both*.

As much as we think we can separate our life experiences by labeling our health, finances, relationships, career and so forth as *parts*, every *part* is having an effect on our entire life experience. Just as each one of us may accept the illusion and believe we are separate from one another, what we do or think also affects the whole, as we are all ONE.

Money as a Spiritual Path

My awareness about money came from growing up in a family that didn't have a lot of it. I was embarrassed. Often my brother and I overheard my parents fighting about money, and I noticed the contrast between *what my family had* and *others who had more*. Although I didn't realize it then, I started creating a story that if we had more money, we'd be happier. It would take years of self-realization, practice and an accumulation of material wealth to realize my misunderstanding.

When I was eight years old, I began working and *making money* by babysitting other people's children. I continually wanted to work and create more financial freedom for myself because of the gap between what I desired and what was actually available for me as a child. Subconsciously, what I was really trying to do was control feelings of sadness, loneliness and fear when my parents were fighting.

I can't remember a time when I didn't work because it was the only way I could have the things my parents didn't provide for me. Even after I was married and had accumulated what I thought would bring me happiness, I realized that there must be something more because I was still feeling sad, lonely and fearful. I had accumulated all of *those things* I thought would *make* me happy, including the nice house, the marriage, the kids, the dogs and family business—but something was still missing. As I became more aware, I gradually realized that *those things* were not what provided happiness for me; I am responsible for my happiness. *Those things* merely gave me more options, comfort and freedom to choose.

Creating freedom for myself has always been the motivating energy propelling me forward.

What I then came to understand was that the energy of money and our relationship to it can be part of our spiritual path and awakening. My relationship with money supported me to realize what is truly important to me: meaningful relationships, feeling spiritually connected, speaking my truth and being authentic in every way, thus creating happiness and financial freedom from the inside-out.

Attracting wealth in the form of money can be part of what supports your awakening.

Creating financial freedom allows you to have more choices and serve more people: This is your Spiritual AND Wealthy invitation.

Everyone Is Spiritual

No matter how *each* of us expresses our personality during this earthly experience, we are all individualized extensions of Divine Energy; thus, we are all *spiritual* beings.

You cannot NOT be spiritual.

This individualized extension of Divine energy is often referred to as the soul or spirit. Because each of is an extension of Spirit, each of us *is* having a spiritual journey. Where we often get stuck is when we judge others and ourselves within the language and agreement of what defines a *spiritual journey* or *spiritual person*. We even attempt to measure *how spiritual* we are in comparison to *how spiritual* others are.

Let me repeat:
You cannot NOT be spiritual.

But why does this matter—really? Your belief or opinion doesn't change the Truth that each person—*everyone, no exceptions*—is an individualized extension of Divine energy, which is the energy of All That Is.

Because every soul is spiritual and every soul is having a spiritual journey, some of the contrast we may observe is whether we or others are *conscious* that we are having this expanded experience we call a *spiritual journey*. Whether we are consciously manifesting our desires, or whether we consistently and consciously focus our thoughts and feelings to align with those desires, *we are all still having a spiritual journey*.

When we consciously create what we desire and align with the highest aspect of ourselves, we feel the love and joy that are our very nature.

You are either creating consciously or creating by egoic default. The degree to which you do either of these is the level of awareness you have in your understanding and remembering that you are Source energy.

Our journey is a continual unlearning and letting go of what *isn't* Source energy. The more each of us expands our awareness and remembers that we *are* Source energy, the more we will embody the higher vibration of all that Source energy *is* and *always has been* within us.

Our conscious spiritual journey is not about measuring or judging whether someone else is consciously awakening. Our conscious spiritual journey is to awaken to our own remembering of who we are and then act from that place of awareness until more awareness is experienced in ongoing waves of ever-expansive energy.

Everyone else's choices and behaviors, conscious or not, are inviting us to awaken to the *truth* that we are and always have been spiritual beings—Divine expressions of Joy and Love. We are here to grow and expand a variety of energies like compassion, Unconditional Love, forgiveness, and so on. There is no finish line where we are complete; there are only ongoing opportunities for Love to expand.

Everything is an Invitation to Love.

For our purpose, your *earthly spiritual journey* is everything your soul experiences from the moment your soul extends into material form through the moment you make your transition and release your physical body. Your soul has always been and will always be experiencing the infinite, which has no boundaries within space and time.

Spiritual Opulence:
Everyone Can Be Wealthy

What does being wealthy mean? Ask a room full of people, and you will find that we all have different definitions of wealth. Yet, no matter what a person's answer may be, when we sift through all the definitions of what each of us is really desiring, the bottom line is that most people feel that if they achieve what defines wealth for them, they would be happy *eventually* or *someday*. However, choosing to delay our happiness by defaulting to *eventually* and *someday* create the ultimate trap and excuse why so many people allow themselves to be unhappy.

Being wealthy is a mindset.

Becoming a wealthy person as well as being OK with defining oneself as wealthy is about taking personal responsibility for creating our own happiness and understanding our freedom to choose. We get to choose how we create our life and how we respond to and think about our life experiences.

Typically, most conversations and definitions about wealth are intertwined with money. So, are the conversations we have about wealth really about money? They can be, if that is what you need and that is where you currently are in your spiritual journey. However, money is not the entirety of the conversation of wealth.

Let me repeat:
True Material Wealth comes from
feeling joyful about what you've created.

There are many people who have accumulated a substantial amount of money, yet they are not necessarily experiencing happiness or creating freedom for themselves. Why is that? Because, again, we need to align our mind with our heart so that we can live from a more elevated understanding of wealth. Through this definition we can individually determine if the current results of our lives are yielding the emotional energy of joy, thus creating energetic freedom.

Regardless of what we have in our bank account, assuming we have one, of course, we need to own and take responsibility for what we are creating through our thoughts and our feelings and then integrate a daily conscious practice to align those thoughts and feelings with what we choose to manifest, whether it's money or something else. Then, we can live a more integrated life of Spiritual Opulence—*the ultimate wealthy existence.*

True Spiritual Wealth + True Material Wealth = Spiritual Opulence

Spiritual AND Wealthy Mindset

Spiritual AND Wealthy people have a deep level of understanding and consistent and active awareness that they, as well as everyone else, are amazing, ever-expanding beings who are here to actualize their unlimited potential, consciously co-creating with the energy of All That Is.

Spiritual AND Wealthy people know there is enough for everyone and are willing to support others to have the opportunity to know the same for themselves.

Spiritual AND Wealthy people know that each individual expression of Divine light is having its own unique spiritual journey. Only when each being is ready can the blossoming of its potential occur. Seeds of awareness must be planted, cultivated and continually harvested during this lifetime and beyond. We cannot force people to realize and actualize their unlimited potential; we can only do this unveiling for ourselves.

What we *can* do, however, as Spiritual AND Wealthy people is to inspire and support others beyond their current awareness. As we share our time, financial resources and the wisdom of what has worked for us, while embracing our passionate work, we can support and inspire others to understand the Divine potential of what is possible for them.

We also understand that we are continually having a human experience, just like everyone else, and that in our human experience we are never done evolving. Spiritual AND Wealthy people know that *every life is perfect*, even though life may not always feel or look perfect for any of us.

Spiritual AND Wealthy people know that everything you need to create is already within you. Your inner journey is to let go of everything that you believe about yourself, others and the world that is *not in alignment* with the energy of Source.

What Are You Wanting to Create?

The freedom to create whatever we want is our natural state of being. Innately, Spiritual AND Wealthy people know we are creators. Freedom to expand energy is what you and I are all about. Any area where we *choose* to focus our attention and expand energetically is ultimately what invites each of us to understand who we are and what we are capable of, as we reawaken the Divinity within.

Would you like more freedom? Where would you want more freedom? Do you feel that attracting more money can support your freedom? Do you want to feel happier or healthier, or attract great love into your life?

For whatever it is you are wanting, you will not be able to attract what you desire until you free yourself from any thoughts, feelings and behaviors that are currently limiting your personal potential. Choose to do something different to free yourself from all limitations so that you can then create the joy, freedom and connection you long for.

The Key to the Keys:
Your Spiritual AND Wealthy Invitation

Be Still in Motion

**Recognition and healing of the illusion of separation
occur as you remember you *are* stillness in motion
and motion within your stillness with All That Is.**

You are not alone.

Surprisingly, I wasn't intuitively guided to write a chapter on meditation as one of the Essential Keys, yet as the book was wrapping up, I kept questioning how the book could be complete without it. How could I not have a meditation chapter in the Essential Keys section? I know, foundationally, that meditation is *the* most essential key to a Spiritual AND Wealthy, joy-filled life.

What was intuitively revealed to me was that meditation is woven throughout the book's Keys—*meditation is the Key to the Keys*. Rather than creating a chapter about meditation as a Key from a place of *egoic* thought and force, I was shown that meditation was already organically integrated into each intuitively created Spiritual AND Wealthy Practice in each Key chapter in this book.

The golden thread that connects all of the Essential Keys is *meditation* or *stillness in motion.*

It was also revealed to me that if meditation as a topic had stood alone as a Key chapter, the word itself might easily trigger resistance based on the reader's ideas and beliefs, thus the possibility of skipping the chapter completely. Instead there is an invitation to a variety of meditative ways we can consciously connect with Spirit; even without a specific meditation chapter, meditation is here, either subtly or obviously.

How we consciously connect is not as important as *just doing it*!

Stillness in Motion

In this human experience, we accumulate many conscious and subconscious beliefs and ways of acting in the world that don't reflect the essence of our Divine self. We downplay who we are and what we are thinking and feeling. Often we ignore what we innately know to be right and true for ourselves, which leads to habits and behaviors that don't match our heart's desires and our loving nature.

Although *how* we developed these habits in the first place can be healing to know, what's more important to know is *how to free ourselves* of any belief or habit delaying us from narrowing the gap between the highest aspect of who we really are and how we are currently expressing ourselves.

Too often we become so focused on *how* we are going to make something happen. In other words, we allow our *egoic* thinking to sabotage our progression because we think we need to *know all the steps along our journey* before we even begin. I like to encourage my clients and audiences *to let go of the how* and concentrate on acknowledging their Divine intuitive nature, while cultivating or expanding their trust and faith with their eternal connection to All That Is. From this place the *how* reveals itself intuitively, step by step, in beautiful, magical and synchronistic ways.

> *How we get to the how* **is through our**
> **ability to create stillness in motion.**

The entirety of how any of us gets from *where we are* to *where we want to be* can be viewed as a movie. There are frames, or stills, within the movie that we can isolate that are glimpses of the entire movie. All we need to do is to *see* and *act* on each frame as we become consciously and more intuitively aware of it as our next step. Each frame is a moment of stillness, yet when we connect each frame, we have an entire moving picture, which is the *how—stillness in motion.*

> **It is only in hindsight that we often see the**
> **connecting frames of our life that have become the**
> **journey of where we are today and how we got here.**

Creating stillness in motion is done in two ways. One way is what we traditionally call meditation. We consciously and deliberately appoint a moment in time to connect with Spirit. My personal knowing is that the ways in which we connect to Spirit through meditation are as limitless as we are. What I also know to be true is that certain styles of meditation work better for some people than others. You may want to experience a variety of meditation styles throughout your journey. A variety may yield better results than becoming dogmatic with a way of meditating that once worked for you but may no longer serve you *now.*

Another way we create stillness in motion is by becoming aware of the moments when we are conscious that we are connected and connecting to Spirit throughout our day. This higher awareness begins to happen for people when they consistently and deliberately schedule time to meditate. The cumulative effect retrains us to remember and then know that we always *have been, are,* and *will be connected* to All That Is.

This time allows us to open ourselves to experiencing the beautiful energy of Unconditional Love, which can initially be overwhelming and uncomfortable because it begins to dissolve our feelings of unworthiness and self-doubt. We can then open to more of an ongoing awareness throughout our day that we are not alone and that we are co-creating each and every minute.

Stillness in motion then becomes a way of life as we bring into fruition consistently throughout our day our deepening awareness of our eternal connection and all that is lovingly offered to us.

Our life becomes an ongoing conversation when we choose to be receptive to the subtle and not-so-subtle ways in which Unconditional Love is demonstrating Presence to us. We become conscious that we are an ongoing, ever-eternal part of the Universal conversation through our stillness in motion or meditative practice.

My Spiritual AND Wealthy invitation to you is to recognize the variety of ways you can consciously connect with Source, and expand your beliefs and experiences beyond needing meditation to *look* or *be* a certain way.

Finding our own way and what works for us individually is in itself a key to our freedom, thus a Spiritual AND Wealthy life where we create more joy in all our life experiences.

If you believe that meditation must completely free your mind or that you are going to be suspended in some state of bliss or nothingness each time you come to your practice, I believe you are setting yourself up for a sense of failure. Haven't most of us had enough opportunities to feel like we haven't done something right? While we can experience ecstatic states of bliss and mindful nothingness during meditation, we can have other infinite experiences that are just as valuable. Ultimately, the intention of our practice is to feel as well as know our Divine connection.

Can freedom from the "monkey mind" be attained? Of course it can. Can we reach states of nothingness and everythingness all at once? Yes, of course.

More importantly, when we allow whatever wants to emerge while we consciously take time to be still and ask clarifying questions, we can create the joy and freedom that we desire. The more we take the time to be still throughout our life, the more easily we can take guided action and connect those "still frames" of ideas and inspirations through our increased intuitive abilities.

We have enough outside influence telling us how every aspect of our life *should be*, which can feel like a daunting task and impossible to achieve. The Keys within this book are intended to be simple, yet rich, invitations to wonder, question and, if nothing else, plant seeds that take you further along your journey.

The Keys provided here are certainly not *all* the Keys to a Spiritual AND Wealthy, joy-filled life. In fact, we often find that there are specific periods in our life where certain Essential Keys will resonate more than others.

These Keys are the only ones I was intuitively guided to share in this book. For example, you will find there is a Key about water yet not a Key specifically about food, which may seem incomplete to you as the reader. Yet, if you allow yourself to look more deeply, food and many other topics are indirectly woven throughout the Keys.

In life we cannot separate one part from any other, and so it is with the Keys. The book is intuitively arranged into these Keys so that you can logically process and integrate each part as you remember *how* to create a more joyful, prosperous and abundant life. Although these Keys are seemingly separate, they do overlap and are interwoven. When you integrate these Essential Keys, you will affect the entirety of your life and create an extraordinary adventure.

Stop Being So Damn Serious and Get Playful: Do Something Extraordinary

There are books I term "lifer" books. These books are worth reading multiple times. I have sometimes felt a nudge, an impulse, to revisit and reread sections or entire books. I have often strategically placed these books in my home so that during more seemingly intense times of opportunities for growth in my life, I have picked one up, fanned the pages with my thumb and stopped where it felt right to do so. I will often *just know* which page to begin reading. It's amazing how often this information is exactly what I needed to hear.

This playful approach is an intuitive way you can use *this* book. When we read a book that has a story line, it makes sense to read from start to finish. *This book is different.*

There is no rule here that you have to proceed in any sequential order or even read this book in its entirety!

Give yourself permission to flip to the contents section and see which Key chapter catches your attention and start there. Or, think of a situation in your life that you would like support and just open the book and read where you feel guided — guilt free.

This book then becomes what the ancients called an *oracle*, one of many ways in which Love speaks to you through a different medium. Using this book, as an oracle is a fun way to use the energy of the wisdom offered here to match an area you are invited to look at to answer your question. Your intention combined with Spiritual Law and Principles will align answers and points to ponder for your expansion.

Why do you think you have this book in your hands? Perhaps in the beginning seeds of new thoughts will be planted and cultivated, and when you are ready, you will reap the benefits of the harvest. Perhaps there is a golden nugget of wisdom waiting for you to have that *ah-ha moment* that propels you forward into a more Spiritual AND Wealthy Life than you are currently living, where *joy* is the ultimate measurement of your Spiritual AND Wealthy Life.

The Essential Spiritual AND Wealthy Keys

I AM
Guided by My Divine Gifts of Intuition

Spiritual AND Wealthy

One

See Your Body as a Living Map

Your body is such a miracle! When we incarnate in this body for the pleasure of our soul's growth and journey, it is like taking a plane or train rather than walking. You chose to grow at a phenomenal speed with the support and assistance that your body provides you in this earthly experience. Your body came equipped with the perfect ability to stay connected with Spirit and receive information to guide you through and toward anything.

The body is a wonderful structure that supports your soul journey and acts like a treasure map. Everything you desire is being supported, directed and attracted through your body. Our work is to know how to read the signs that come to and through our body, no different than reading the legend on a map.

Intuition is the ability to receive support and guidance and remember that we are connected to All That Is. Everyone, *without exception*, has intuitive capabilities. I see these abilities as a living map that allows each of us to receive guidance not only with practical, daily choices but also with the manifestation of our larger, overall goals, dreams and visions.

Through our intuitive abilities, we are first shown these dreams and visions to inspire us to reveal the greatness that lives within each of us. Our dreams and desires invite us to reach higher and become more than we think we are able to achieve or what we think we deserve.

Our intuition is far beyond how we think or what we consider logical. Once you tap into this natural resource, however, you will begin to see an increase in the synchronistic events of people, places and things in your life. You can deepen your awareness and commitment to using this natural gift to actualize the greatest potential that is within you.

When we wonder how we are going to make our dreams come true or where to start to achieve them, we only need to develop, trust and act on the guidance we receive intuitively, which then allows what seems like magic to happen in our life.

There are multi-dimensional ways you sense and receive intuitive guidance internally and externally through your body. For example, we can "see" not only externally through our physical eyes but also internally through our "third eye," or what some call the "mind's eye." For simplicity and the purpose of this book, we will focus on the following four typical intuitive abilities, which you will be invited to investigate more in this chapter's Spiritual AND Wealthy Practice section:

Clairvoyance: Intuitive visual guidance
Clairaudience: Intuitive auditory guidance
Clairsentience: Intuitive sensory guidance
Claircognizance: Intuitive knowing guidance

As you become more conscious about these abilities, you may notice that one of these gifts feels more natural than the others because it is innately stronger for you. However, all of these intuitive gifts can be developed as much or as little as you choose to expand them.

Trusting and taking action as intuitively guided creates more ease and grace in your life. For example, when we have a gut feeling and *trust it,* and we do something because of that information, we often prevent something from happening we would want to avoid, or we feel confident we are doing the right thing.

When we have *not trusted* that information and ignored that inner knowing or feeling, we generally experience a sense of regret, knowing we should have done something different. We have all experienced something that didn't turn out well, and we often said something like "I had a feeling," "I knew that was going to happen," or "I knew I should/shouldn't have done that." This is self-betrayal.

Betraying ourselves creates extraordinary pain and suffering along our journey. Most people have the deepest pain and regret where they have betrayed themselves by ignoring the intuitive information they've received. I invite you, like my clients, to forgive any area in your life where you have betrayed yourself. I teach my clients to be more obedient to their inner voice, and I encourage you to do the same.

Intuition is the portal to everything you want.

As we listen to our intuition, we betray ourselves less and start loving ourselves more. As we allow this loving guidance system to support our life, we create more joy, prosperity and abundance. Trusting and tuning into our intuition is the most important, foundational wisdom I teach my clients.

Initially, I help clients to understand their primary—or innate—intuitive gift, the one that comes the easiest to them. Then, as we work together, they gain more confidence to practice, expand and integrate all four intuitive abilities.

As the spiritual muscle of intuition is flexed and developed through *trust* and *action*, you can begin to amalgamate your gifts of clairvoyance, clairaudience, clairsentience and claircognizance more often and with greater speed. Intuitive guidance then becomes a conscious, confident, co-creative part of our journey, which is exactly how it was intended all along.

▲ Universal Wisdom

You were given everything you needed for your journey.

I AM

▲ **Spiritual AND Wealthy Practice**

Everyone has these four main, multi-dimensional ways that they receive intuitive guidance internally and externally—you are no exception.

Throughout your day, pay attention to how your body is communicating what you need to know. Remember that one of these gifts may feel more natural for you; however, with your intention, all of these gifts can be expanded.

1. Notice anything you are visually drawn to or that you see repeatedly in your mind's eye.

Clairvoyance is the most common and easiest way most people receive messages from Spirit.

2. Notice anything you hear inside or outside your head that has a positive, directive message about your prayers or intentions.

If you are unsure that what you are hearing through your clairaudience is ego or Spirit, ask Spirit for confirmation.

3. Notice anything you are feeling in your body.

The most common experience people have is chills or goose bumps that radiate throughout their body. Confirmation often comes to people this way as well as feeling the joyful presence of Spirit. These and other feelings invite us to stay present in the moment and pay attention to what is happening.

4. Notice anything that comes to you as a knowing without any evidence—you just know.

Claircognizance is your ability to know things without knowing how you know. Start noticing the seemingly little things like when your phone rings, and you know who it is.

5. Educate yourself.

You can read, listen to audio programs, or hire an intuitive coach to learn to trust and practice using your Divine gifts of intuition. We are so blessed to live in a time of great resources. Utilize a variety of these resources for your spiritual study and allow more prosperity to flow into every area of your life by listening to your body, and experiencing it as a living map to support you.

♥ BONUS: My Gift for You

In support of your journey, I have a free gift for you, which will further open your intuitive abilities and help support your Spiritual AND Wealthy life.

Please go to the following link for my gift for you:
http://angelsandprosperity.com/spiritualandwealthybookgift

I AM
Stillness

Spiritual AND Wealthy

Two

Be One with Your Water

Water is the stream of life on this planet. It flows to you and through you, transforming with you. We have harnessed the power of water in many of our societies. Yet, many of us have forgotten how important water is for our physical body and equally how important it is for our spiritual well-being.

Water is the body's principal chemical component and is approximately 60 percent of your body weight. Various organs, such as the heart and brain, contain much higher percentages of water. Your body is a Divine instrument, the vehicle in which your Divine essence experiences this manifested reality.

Just as a musician would maintain a musical instrument, keeping your body fine-tuned will allow you to use all the gifts your body has to offer you along your journey, including but not limited to your intuitive capacities, cognitive thinking, motor skills, energy levels and detoxification. All instruments and vehicles require the ideal care and maintenance to perform optimally, and your body is no exception.

Creating a Spiritual AND Wealthy life is a series of simple, daily practices that when implemented collectively and consistently allow you to be the best *you* possible on a multitude of levels.

One of the ways to support your *body, mind, and spirit experience* is to incorporate drinking ideal amounts of water that are right for you as a daily spiritual practice.

Drinking water as a spiritual practice may sound odd. I consistently find that people who feel like they are disconnected spiritually, stuck in their lives, not thinking clearly and physically unwell are more often than not *dehydrated on a regular basis.* Dehydration has become a normal way of living, but it is not a healthy way of living, nor is it ideal.

We begin learning early in life to ignore the wisdom of our body, often starting with the grade school environment. Taking the time and having the ability to hydrate throughout the day is not encouraged in the classroom to the degree that would actually benefit the individual learning experience. Often we are not respected for honoring what our body needs. Asking in front of our classmates to use the toilet or get a drink when we need to can initiate questions about the necessity from the teacher—"Do you really need to go? Can't you wait?"

Some of us begin to drink less because we feel embarrassed with this focused attention, and we subconsciously learn to conform to unhealthy norms. Unfortunately, this pattern often continues into adulthood, and we stop listening to our body's wisdom in other areas of our life as well.

More than 75% of my new clients are not adequately hydrated. Often, the very first time I speak with a new client to schedule their appointment, I am intuitively shown that they are dehydrated. I immediately encourage clients to get hydrated by drinking more water to prepare for our session and begin a healthy and healing habit of self-loving care.

As one of my dearest friends says, "I am not a doctor, nor do I play one on TV." Neither am I. I can tell when you are hydrated or not, but I can't determine the adequate amount of water your body needs.

I highly recommend that you check with your doctor or health care practitioner to know how much water is perfect for your build, your current level of activity, your health, as well as the climate you live in. Bottom line here: When your urine has a strong odor and is dark in color, it is very likely you are dehydrated.

When you take good care of yourself even with the simple act of staying hydrated, you are proclaiming, "I value my body, and I am worthy of experiencing a joyful, healthy and prosperous life." Drinking water to stay hydrated is a great act of self-love.

We often subconsciously make things complicated and hard. Keep it simple: Add adequate amounts of water throughout the day and notice the uplifting effects it has on your overall well-being.

▲ Universal Wisdom

Your reflection is found in the sanctity and qualities of water.

▲ Spiritual AND Wealthy Practice

1. Know how much water is right for you.

A very general guideline is an 8-ounce glass, 8 times per day. Find out what is right for you and educate yourself on the signs and symptoms of what even mild dehydration look like so that you can keep that wonderful and unique body fine-tuned.

2. Get visual about your water.

Every morning measure out the full amount of water that is right for you in one or two CLEAR containers. Keep the containers in view so that you can clearly see throughout the day how you are doing with your water intake and adjust accordingly.

3. Start your day in the flow.

I recommend getting in the habit of drinking a full glass of water right after you get out of bed. This practice will give your body, mind, and spirit a great start. Your body has been intelligently repairing and restoring all night and needs more than food or caffeinated beverages to start your day.

3. Get your guzzle on.

When you do take a drink of water, take in a nice volume of water. Little sips here and there will rarely get you to your daily water goal.

4. Trust your inner guidance about caffeine.

When you drink beverages other than water, choose beverages that keep you hydrated more than caffeinated beverages do. If you choose caffeinated beverages, that's okay; just make a mental note to compensate for that by drinking extra water or eating more juicy fruits and vegetables.

5. Drink at regular intervals throughout the day.

When you set specific, consistent times throughout the day to hydrate, your body's cell memory will begin to kick in over time so that your water practice becomes a healthy and loving habit.

6. Keep your blood sugar levels up.

When you are tired or sluggish during the day, drinking more water will help restore you. Often people reach for the sugary snack and a caffeinated beverage. Although these things may be yummy and feel good for the moment, they will not sustain you energetically as well a healthy snack and an 8-ounce glass of water will.

7. Bless your water.

Take a moment before you drink to give thanks for the water while setting an intention that the water nourishes and brings all aspects of you into perfect health and spiritual alignment.

8. Increase your vibration with the vibration of the water you drink.

In his book, <u>The Hidden Messages in Water</u>, Dr. Masaru Emoto verified in his experiments how we actually change the crystalline shape of water molecules with the use of positive words.

As we change the crystalline structure of our water we raise our vibration. We can actually make the crystalline structure of our water more beautiful—think of the gorgeous symmetry of snowflakes. Imagine that you are drinking beautiful snowflakes!

▲*What high-vibrating words would you like to infuse into your water?*

▲*Do you desire to be more loving or bring more love into your life?*

Then, write "Love" or "I AM Love" or any positive words on your water container.

Every day write positive, high-vibrating words on the container you keep your water in or place your hands on the container while intending beautiful ideas and words to be carried within the crystalline structure of your water. This practice blesses your water, supporting your energetic shift and daily spiritual growth. You are actually creating Holy water and gifting yourself a blessing.

I AM
Divine Royalty

Spiritual AND Wealthy

Three

Restore Your Divine Inheritance by Receiving

Your Divine nature is to give and receive Love. Love expresses itself in a multitude of ways, from a compliment to a job promotion, from a friend picking up the check to someone opening the door for you. The ability to receive must be balanced with our ability to give: *This is Divine Law.*

Everything has contrasting, balancing energy. The contrasting, balancing energies bring us variety in our life experience. We have night and day, salty and sweet, inhaling and exhaling, high tides and low tides, as well as other infinite contrasting examples of balanced energy.

Divine Source energy reveals to us from the very beginning of our physical journey the important nature of receiving, by intending it to be *the very first thing we experience* outside of our mother's womb. We must be both *willing* and *able* to receive or "take" our first breath; *our soul will not experience life in human form here on Earth without first receiving.* We balance the first breath we receive with the last breath we exhale as we complete our life cycle, releasing our soul essence from our earthly experience.

Everything in this life experience has a giving and a receiving quality to it, and without these two contrasting Divine essences, our

I AM

life is not in harmony or balance because *both* need to be equally valued as a practice. If you tend to give more than you receive, you will create disharmony in your ability to manifest. Manifestation is the ability to transform non-material energy into material by energetically saying, "Yes" to it by your consistent, focused thoughts and feelings.

Unfortunately, we may have learned along our journey that it is better to give than receive. You may have been told that you are greedy if you want or desire more than someone else has. This mindset is actually preventing you from receiving the very experiences you desire while limiting your ability to serve others in a bigger way.

I've noticed that my clients who struggle with receiving tend to also have unsatisfying financial income. When they allow themselves to receive in more areas of their life, they can increase their opportunities to attract and receive more money, creating more financial freedom and the ability to impact others more generously with their time and money.

I understand there are many positive intentions behind the saying, "It is better to give than receive." A Spiritual AND Wealthy mindset sees the act of being able to give and being able to receive as two sides of the same coin. You can't give anything to anyone unless there is someone willing to receive it. Both *are* of equal value.

**If everyone is giving because it is better,
then who is going to receive if it is not equally valued?**

If you believe giving has a higher value over receiving, then you, like many people, are off course in the direction of your dreams. Are people not as good because they are on the receiving end of the giving? Subconsciously, what we inherently learn is that someone who receives is not as good as someone who gives.

It is better to give AND to receive.

We need to see our receiving nature as naturally as our birthright to breathe. Do you walk around saying, "I wonder if I am worthy to breathe today?" No, you just do it naturally. When you see and value receiving as your Divine inheritance as a gift, you will begin to heal your individual wounds around unworthiness as well as contribute to healing the collective wounds around unworthiness.

When we are offered something like a simple compliment, we don't often welcome and receive the heartfelt praise—energetically, we are saying "No" to Spirit. We are often taught to politely say "thank you," but in general many people brush off praise because they don't understand that receiving the compliment supports the healing of the illusion of unworthiness and the ability to manifest their desires.

I hear many women, for example, not accept compliments as though they were batting a fly away. When complimented about their clothes, they quickly respond by saying their outfit is old or that it was on sale.

Can you imagine saying "no thanks" to Love? Just for a moment, personify God in human form and imagine "him" or "her" showing up at your door with a gift, and you don't even open the door. Maybe you open the door, but then you close the door right in God's face. Silly example maybe, but that is exactly what you do when you are not restoring your Divine Inheritance by receiving *all* Divine gifts, including something you may see as simple as a compliment.

Everything comes from Divine Source energy. When we minimize what we consider to be a simple compliment, we are saying "no" to the flow of love that Spirit is sending our way through a variety of people, places and experiences, which essentially are inviting us to heal and understand our innate goodness and worth.

Receiving invites you to acknowledge that you are a special and glorious light being of royal heritage. It requires you to let go of what anyone else thinks about you and your desires. It requires you to commit to being self-aware when something as *simple* as a compliment comes your way or when a friend expects to buy you lunch. Your "yes" or "no" affects prosperity in all areas of your life.

In each and every moment, your Spiritual AND Wealthy invitation is to receive all Divine gifts that present themselves so that you can then actualize all of the money, relationships, radiant health or any joyful experience you desire.

▲ Universal Wisdom

Love continues to express itself towards you and then through you to restore your collective memory of wholeness.

▲ Spiritual AND Wealthy Practice

1. Begin your day in wonder and expectation.

Before you get out of bed in the morning, say to yourself, "I wonder what gifts of Love will be offered to me today?" Next, reach your hands up to the sky and say, "Spirit, I am open to receive love from you in any and all creative ways today."

2. Notice the gifts you receive each day.

Become aware of all the ways in which this beautiful Divine Universe loves you throughout your day, making itself known through synchronistic experiences.

3. Breathe in what you receive.

When you are offered love in any form, take a moment before you speak or do anything and receive a very deep inhalation. This breathing practice allows you to anchor in the ability to receive, which transforms unhealthy patterns of rejecting love into healthy patterns of receiving love.

4. Give thanks for what you receive.

Just say "thank you," clean and simple.

Often when someone gifts us something, we say too many things that can take away from the Love that desires to express in that moment.

5. Choose to receive.

The choice to receive presents itself multiple times everyday. Your inner transformation happens each time you say "yes" to Love in the variety of ways it is offered to you.

I AM
Always Supported by Love

Spiritual AND Wealthy

Four

Ask for Help

Our human experience is full of "ups" and "downs." Each one of us has our own tipping point of how many *down* experiences we can handle before we feel overwhelmed, stuck or even hopeless. Asking for help is key for creating more *up* experiences than *down* ones.

Source energy is always available to support you through friends, loved ones, strangers, as well as the invisible realm of Spirit. If you have a hard time asking for help from those around you, it is likely you are also not asking for help from the spiritual realm. Successful people ask for help.

Asking for help can be very uncomfortable for many because we judge it as a sign of weakness or feel unworthy. Seeking help is really a point of strength, courage and your true nature as a co-creative being.

We were never meant to *do this* alone.

The lie that we are all separate beings lures us into thinking we have to be able to "do it all" on our own. All successful people have had some level of support from others to reach their goals and dreams. When you try to go it alone, you will often feel inadequate and frustrated in the process. For many people, requesting help only comes

I AM

when they have reached bottom. You will experience more peace in your life when you consistently ask for support from both spiritual and earthly sources throughout your journey.

You have never been and will never be alone. The Divine plan is for you to have a team of loving spiritual beings available to be of service to you every minute of the day. Each of us is surrounded by the energy of angels, ascended masters, guides, saints and dearly departed loved ones—and so much more than we can fully comprehend. These energetic extensions of Source energy are closer than our breath and often answer our questions before we finish our sentences. I call this team of Love *my peeps* or *my entourage* and encourage you to recognize that you also have your own team.

Spirit is always supporting us by matching our thoughts and feelings. When we get conscious about creating at a high level, all we need to do is ask for assistance. Our free will is never usurped by Spirit so, when we consciously ask for support, we create at a much higher frequency within us, and we begin to allow more Love to flow to us and through us.

The request for help from Source energy gives us an opportunity to prevent or shift our experiences of lower vibrations. We can then move into and sustain a higher frequency, creating prosperity in the areas we allow ourselves to be supported.

When we ask for help, we innately know that a solution exists.

With each request for help we begin to recognize the infinite possibilities that are available to us. We honor ourselves, and we honor others, as we seek support. We demonstrate self-love and remind others that they can do the same.

When we ask for help through prayer, what we are really asking for is the reflection and amplification of what already exists in us, such as courage, compassion, forgiveness and strength, to radiate through us. "God give me the strength" then becomes "God remind me of the strength that already lies within me."

You can begin to see yourself as part of the whole connected to everything, when you ask for help, when you hire help, and when you pray for help. This allows you to step out of the illusion of separation and into the truth, experiencing yourself as Oneness Consciousness.

No request for help is too big or too small.

It is our judgment about what we deem important or worthy that often stops us from asking for help. *To Spirit it is all worthy.* So, stop judging and start asking for help.

It is our Divine nature to be of service to others.

You deprive others of the ability to extend their Divine essence to you by being of service when you don't ask for their help. Allowing help and assistance into your life is a gift to yourself and others. Asking for help will set in motion a ripple of prosperous energy because you align yourself in the balanced energy of giving and receiving.

▲ **Universal Wisdom**

All energetic alignment for manifestation of the invisible into visible is from the co-creation of multiple energies within the whole.

▲ **Spiritual AND Wealthy Practice**

1. Recognize that you have Spiritual support at all times.

Begin your day by asking that Spirit reveal itself to you throughout your day through signs, symbols, people and experiences that you will easily recognize.

2. Ask Spirit to reveal your next step, a solution or a different way to look at any situation.

Take all your cares, worries and concerns to Spirit as well as your hopes, dreams and desires. There is support for all areas of your life, and no part of your life is off-limits to ask for help.

3. When you feel the need or desire to reach out to others for help, take action without delay.

Trust that this feeling to ask for help is an answer and solution to the particular need or desire you are having. Too often we have an urge to ask for support from friends or family, but we stop ourselves. We often decide for others, rather than allowing them the opportunity to say "yes" or "no" to us.

4. Gather a team of support for your Spiritual AND Wealthy life.

Successful people have a team that supports them. Look at Oprah; she is successful for two major reasons. First, she knows her connection to Spirit is foundational to her personally and professionally. Second, she surrounds herself with a team of people to support her both personally and professionally. She started with limited help and gathered her team along the way. You can gather your team, too.

5. Gift someone the opportunity to give to you.

Think back to a time when you were happy that someone asked you for help, and you found pleasure in supporting him/her. Allow someone to do this for you.

6. Let go of perfectionism and delegate.

Get real and be honest. There are things you are doing that someone else could do. Make lists of areas in your life that only you can do and then areas that someone else can do. Creating these lists can be a challenge for those of you who feel the need to control, but I promise that you will feel a greater sense of well-being and control when you let go and let others do the best job they can for you.

Attempting to do it all yourself is virtually impossible, so ask for help: hire someone, get an intern—just do something differently so that you can create more possibilities and freedom in your life.

I AM
Willing

Spiritual AND Wealthy

Five

Embrace and Celebrate Resistance

I have very good news for you about the energy of resistance: Resistance is *natural,* and resistance has a *purpose.* Our Spiritual AND Wealthy invitation is to rewire our thinking about what resistant energy is all about so that we can embrace it, move more gracefully through it, and celebrate it.

You can create a *huge shift in consciousness* when you welcome resistance. The truth about resistance is that each of us has experienced it and may continue to experience it. We mostly experience negative effects and feelings about resistance until we learn to shift our perspective, language and beliefs.

If you have ever said or felt like you were *blocked, struggling, overwhelmed, defiant, sad, angry, fearful or terrified,* or any variation of these feelings, you were most likely experiencing some level of resistance to what was happening in your life or what was wanting to manifest through you.

Most people experience resistance as being very uncomfortable. Some of you might agree that *uncomfortable* is putting it mildly. Perhaps some of you have experienced resistance as *complete and utter terror* like I have in the past. If you have ever experienced a panic attack, or know someone who has, that would be an extremely high level of resistance being experienced.

My clients are often shocked by my reaction when they tell me, "I am really struggling right now" or "I feel stuck." My usual response is "great" or "good," because I know that when we get support to shift the feelings and the energy of resistance, we can get to the other side of the uncomfortable energy often faster than we can do it alone. Either way, one must be willing to shift his/her beliefs and perspectives to see the beauty that can be found at looking and exploring resistance in a new way.

The degree to which you are experiencing resistance
is the degree to which *you* are calling forth
your own soul's growth and expansion.

There is GOLD waiting to be discovered on the other side of whatever is being experienced when you move through and embrace any resistance you are feeling. Keeping a journal often helps us to see how much more conscious we have become on our journey.

Our resistance often reveals previously
held wounds ready to be healed.

I recommend journaling about how you're feeling, and I invite you to set an intention within your writing to connect your current experiences and feelings to a past wound with the intention of clearing and releasing the attached energy.

We are calling forth the very things we are experiencing. Since we are consistently creating our own reality, when you are resisting, the question becomes "What desires to be expressed through me?" When we are willing to ask questions and use our attention to focus on our spiritual growth, we have the possibility of discovering the gold.

We begin to bring relief to ourselves, and we become less fearful, less blocked, less sad and so on. The investigation itself begins the process of letting go, which forms the foundation of our spiritual growth. We have continual opportunities to allow new ways of our soul's expression to emerge.

Every consistent prayer, intention, meditation, thought and feeling you have is calling something into manifested form. So, when you can embrace that you called something into being and then learn to dance with it rather than run from it, you will eventually get to the other side of the experience that is seeking you and that you are seeking. You will also begin to see that you have *allowed* more of your *authentic self* to emerge because of it.

Often people call times of resistance "The Dark Night of the Soul," our feeling of being disconnected from Spirit. Although it's impossible to actually be disconnected from Spirit, we may *feel* that we are alone and without light. The dark night of the soul can be experienced for days, weeks or even years. The length of time depends on how much focus we give to the light energy that wants to emerge or how much focused attention we give to the dark that is being allowed to live and magnify in our space.

**The more conscious we become, the more we remember
our innate wisdom that we really are never alone.
This is awakening.**

When we are resisting, we are in a temporary state in which we just can't perceive the light that is always there. Shifting our current line of vision and perspective then becomes key.

**When we are willing to embrace *the dark night of
the soul* as being the *bearer of the light*, then and only
then can we exponentially shift our resistant energy
into the vibrant frequency of anticipatory celebration.**

▲ Universal Wisdom

Until you learn to measure your growth in celebratory energy, you will utilize the contrasting energy of resistance and surrender to measure your individualized growth.

▲ Spiritual AND Wealthy Practice

Positively shift your energy and perspective of resistance with the following *writing and reflective* practices.

1. Choose an area of your life where you are feeling frustration, hurt, sadness, unforgiveness, anger or any kind of limiting energy.

2. Once you've chosen an area where you'd like to shift your energy, you can evaluate your current level of resistance, using the following approach.

This practice offers your logical mind the opportunity to measure the potential growth opportunity so that you can positively reframe something viewed as a problem and transmute the energy into what your heart and soul know is an invitation to freedom.

Using a scale between 1 and 100, where 1 represents little to no resistance, and 100 represents completely stuck energy and feelings of terror, complete the following.

▲*In order to imagine your current level of resistance with the area you chose, picture a pole in front of you. One (1) will be at the bottom and 100 at the top. Ask your highest self to reveal to you where your current level of resistant energy is. You may see an indication of your current resistant vibration by seeing a number as a percentage, a marker along the pole at a certain level between the 1 and 100. You may have an inner knowing of what your number is. Trust your first impression and don't edit yourself.*

▲*Once you have your number, relate it to how you have been feeling and open your heart and mind to align to this expansive growth opportunity. A larger number means you have probably been experiencing intense limiting energy around your area of concern, where the opposite is true with a smaller number. The higher the number, the greater the expansive growth opportunity is before you.*

Remember that the highest aspect of you does not see or feel any area in your life as a problem or painful situation; it only sees an opportunity for you to remember who you truly are by coming into alignment and taking you from where you are to where your highest self is. It is merely your egoic personality self that sees any area of your life as negative.

▲*Now make a conscious choice. Receive a deep breath and ask yourself, "Do I expect to see this area as a positive opportunity to grow and expand, or do I want to stay where I am and continue to see and experience the constricting energy, knowing that I will continue to create more suffering for myself?"*

3. Take the following steps to move the resistant energy.

You are invited to see this area as a positive opportunity to grow and shift the current limiting energy you are experiencing into expansive energy.

▲*How do you want to feel when you are on the other side of this experience? Capture that feeling by imagining it now.*

▲*What can you imagine you might learn from this opportunity? If you had to guess, what is the first thought that comes to mind?*

▲*What higher qualities of being are being called forth? What are the qualities within you that might be expanded as you reach the other side of your opportunity to grow? Will you be more courageous, forgiving or authentic?*

▲*What do you need to let go of to step into this experience and move through it with more ease and grace?*

I AM

▲Can you see any reasons why this experience might be revealing itself to you now?

▲What is one practical step you could take right now that could make a difference in moving forward vs. staying right where you are?

▲Whom could you ask for help, both in the physical world and spiritual realm?

> *Taking steps, having a plan, and giving our mind something else to do will bring relief. We only need a little relief to begin to move what feels like a mountain of resistance.*

4. Receive a breath to anchor your willingness to shift your energy with what you've just completed.

Now, re-imagine what it will feel like to be on the other side of this opportunity and growth experience. Complete this practice by receiving another breath, trusting you have expanded your energy.

Smile. ☺

I AM
the Word

Spiritual AND Wealthy

Six

Choose Your Words Wisely

Everything that you communicate through the spoken or written word creates an impact on you, others and the world. You can easily assess the quality and impact your words are having by the results you are currently experiencing in your life.

Each and every word holds a very specific frequency. The combinations of words you weave together in conversation collectively create vibrations and specific tones that orchestrate the quality of *all* your life experiences.

All words are powerful. All words you communicate create change and impact, even if no one else sees or hear them. We often think that the quiet words we say only to ourselves don't really matter, but they do. Everything is vibration, including our words. Each of us is a musical instrument, creating a tone and contributing our unique expression to the collective vibration of all.

Some individual words as well as combinations of words are more powerful and harmonious than others. The most powerful combination of words you can use is "I AM" and anything following these words. "I" represents the true essence of your very being as an individual extension of creative Divine energy, while "AM" represents the command or action that is being summoned by that creative Divine energy to take action with whatever words follow "I AM."

Therefore, when you say, "I AM," followed by "broke this month," you activate your Divine creative essence and command the vibration and manifestation of being without enough money.

I AM + "broke this month" = not enough $$$

Source energy will always align with what you consistently focus on—whether your energy is focused on something you want or the very things you say you don't want. What tips the scale in one direction or the other in what you manifest resides in where you consistently vibrate through your words, thoughts and feelings.

Your words create vibration whether someone actually hears them or reads them. Your thoughts, formed by words, create physical, mental and emotional vibrations within you, which become your points of attraction for creating in material form.

Henry Ford understood the energy and power of our words and subsequently our thoughts when he said, "Whether you think that you can, or that you can't, you are usually right."

The most magical transformation occurs when we speak from a place of what we want, rather than continually declaring what we don't want.

Many people have learned to connect with each other by focusing their conversation around their challenges and negative news. This approach keeps us small and stuck, and gives many people a false sense of connection and community. We reinforce the collective consciousness of unworthiness, creating lack and limitation, when we continue to minimize what is wonderful in our lives.

Because we have learned to connect with people through the negative, we often don't allow ourselves to focus on or speak about the simple pleasures in our life. We will, however, give ourselves and others permission to discuss "the less frequent big things" like weddings, bar mitzvahs and births. Our Spiritual AND Wealthy invitation is to focus our daily conversations on the simple joys of our lives so that we can create more things to be joyful about.

If you expect something to be different, you need to declare from the vision of what is possible, *not* from your current results or other people's limited beliefs. Anything you're experiencing currently in your life is the result of your previous, most repeated declarations — positive or negative.

We need to shift our mindset, our beliefs and our focus to speak and think from a place of what we expect to manifest. Often this shift feels like a lie to people because the results of their lives feel more real than the true reality of their Divine vision.

You are a co-creator of your reality here on Earth.

For example, financially successful people who came from a background of poverty became successful financially by continually affirming their Divine vision of wealth. Instead of complaining how poor they were, they began to speak, feel and act from the place they expected to be — and they continue to do so.

You cannot continue to focus your thoughts and words on what's not working in your life and expect to create what you desire.

Choosing our words wisely and shifting our focus from *what is* to *what we want* is not always the easiest in the beginning. While you may want a quick fix and fast results, the magic is in the consistency and quality of the words you are speaking, which are creating your future and your freedom.

▲ Universal Wisdom

All is made manifest for you with your command. As you command consistently and with expectancy, you create an energetic charge that eventually creates a tipping point and thus manifests results you will decide are in your favor or not. You then can clarify your command to manifest more precise results.

▲ Spiritual AND Wealthy Practice

1. Believe that your words have power and substance.

The words you choose create your thoughts and feelings; your thoughts and feelings create your reality — this is basic yet powerful spiritual principle.

2. Set an intention to have a heightened awareness of what you are communicating as well as what is being communicated around you.

Noticing what you and others are saying and creating will allow you to be more conscious of what you may need to reframe to create what you desire.

3. Reframe or shift the statements you notice create opposition to what you desire.

Remember that we shift by declaring and expecting what we desire, not what is showing up right now.

For example, if you notice you are saying, "I AM sad," you perpetuate that the essence of who you are, as sadness, which is not true. You also continue to manifest more things to feel sad about. Rather than declaring you are sad, you can honor that you're experiencing the emotion of sadness by saying, "Although I feel sad in this moment, I know from previous experience that this feeling is temporary — this too shall pass."

Although you may not instantaneously feel better, affirming something like the following repeatedly can move you in the direction of feeling joy: "I AM Divine Joy, and I now allow this to express fully through me, as me."

With the expectancy of shifting a lower feeling vibration, I often repeat the same I AM statement over and over again until I feel some measure of relief.

4. Create, declare and command your future results through writing and displaying positive "I AM" statements that reflect your most current desires.

Get inspired from the following examples.

▲*If you're currently not experiencing radiant health, and that is what you desire, consistently say or write one of the following statements:*

"*I AM radiant health.*"

"*I AM perfectly aligned with the Divine wisdom of my body.*"

▲*If you're currently not experiencing harmony in your relationships, consistently say or write the following:*

"*I AM harmony in all of my relationships.*"

"*I AM harmonizing energy in my relationship with _____.*"

▲*If you're currently not experiencing confidence in trusting your intuition, consistently say or write the following:*

"*I AM obedient to the voice of my soul.*"

5. Once daily, speak aloud the words "I AM" seven times.

Inhale and exhale after stating each "I AM." You may feel lighter or have a sense of subtle to powerful energy throughout your body.

Inhale.

Without exhaling, say, "I AM."

Then, exhale.

Repeat this cycle at least six more times.

I AM
Harmonious Action

Spiritual AND Wealthy

Seven

Start Creating Contribution and Stop Creating Contamination

I have often contemplated how we could make better use of the words *love* and *fear* to guide our choices, and then along came the words *Contribution* and *Contamination* to show me a new way. When I heard these words from Glenn Morshower, I knew in that moment that these words would change my life and also the way I would teach about love and fear.

As we become more conscious of our spiritual journey, we may begin to hear and read the words *love* and *fear* through spiritual communities, books and teachings. Yet often we are unable to truly integrate and utilize these words to consistently better our lives. It's as though we give these words "lip service," but we're not truly integrating them as a daily spiritual practice to make better choices to create what we desire.

We are here to love as well as free ourselves from any fears of acting from a space of love in all we do.

Integrating *Contribution* [love] and *Contamination* [fear] as inquiry can align your life with Love, shake you to the core of your being and wake you up more than any other words I know — even *love* and *fear*. We simply need to ask, "Does it [my words, action, reaction] Contribute or Contaminate?" *We can't easily negotiate or play egoic mind games as we utilize these words.* What you are creating in your life then becomes crystal clear as you answer these questions.

Your Spiritual AND Wealthy invitation is to gift yourself the ability to be 100% responsible for what you are creating, whether you like what is showing up or not. You can always create something new. When you ask, "Does it Contribute or Contaminate?" you create a pinpoint moment — what I call the *Holy Second* — where you consciously choose to continue with the creative energy you are expressing or to shift it.

There are 86,400 *Holy Seconds* in every 24-hour period of your day, which is a heck of a lot of opportunity to quickly assess and know instantly that you can do something different in order to move forward in a space of *Love* and *Contribution*.

As a bottom-line kind of gal, I gravitate towards anything that simplifies my life and helps me create less chaos, pain and suffering while creating more peace, joy and freedom. Applying the words *Contribution* and *Contamination* to simplify your life and your choices can create the same peace, joy and freedom for you.

Ultimately, we can use the words *Contribution* and *Contamination* as spiritual tools to assess anything and everything we are up to, have been up to or will be up to. Super simple.

Let me offer you an example.

You just received your credit card bill, and it is a bit higher than you were consciously aware it would be. How you feel when you open that bill, what you say to yourself internally or to others externally, how you use the credit card in the future, how you choose to pay it down or off, for example, will create an energetic flow that *Contaminates* or *Contributes* to your life.

Let's say you obsessively think about your credit card bill as a debt that is now *weighing you down*.

Then... **You are creating Contamination.**

Let's say you decide to take the credit card out of your wallet and put it away until it is paid off and only use cash.

Then... **You are creating Contribution.**

Let's say you complain to your friends or family about not being able to do things until you pay off your credit card.

Then... **You are creating Contamination.**

What if you play a game with yourself and see how quickly you can creatively pay down the bill without even knowing how it will happen?

Then... **You are creating Contribution.**

As you move forward from this moment, you can gain new perspective and value by reviewing your past and current results in any area of your life. Ask yourself the following simple questions about an area of your life where you're currently experiencing some level of pain:

✓ Has what you *have done* created Contribution or Contamination?

✓ Is what you *are doing* Contributing or Contaminating?

✓ Will what you *are going to do* Contribute or Contaminate?

You have the choice to do things differently at any time. It doesn't matter what you've done or what you're currently doing.

What matters now is what you're going to do.

▲ Universal Wisdom

Everything you are wanting and everything that you are is Love and from a vibration of Love. To be, do or say anything to the contrary creates pain and suffering within you.

▲ Spiritual AND Wealthy Practice

1. Consider any area in your life where you are currently experiencing any pain or suffering.

Write your answers to the following questions regarding this area you're considering.

▲*Is what I am saying to myself about _____ Contributing or Contaminating?*

▲*What can I say to myself that would Contribute to what I am really wanting with _____?*

▲*What do I typically say in verbal or written form to others about _____? Do these words Contribute or Contaminate?*

▲*What could I do differently in how or what I communicate to others about _____ so that I could Contribute to what I am really wanting?*

▲*What is one thing I could stop doing with _____ that would Contribute to what I am really seeking?*

▲*What is one action that I have been resisting that I could now take with* _____ *that would Contribute to what I desire?*

▲*Is there something I need to stop doing regarding* _____ *and other areas of my life so that I will transform the Contamination energy into Contribution energy?*

These are a small sample of possible questions that you can use to support yourself in any area of your life. Change them or create new ones, using appropriate versions of Contaminate and Contribute, such as Contamination, Contribution, Contaminating and Contributing.

2. Be conscious of who you are allowing to *Contribute* to your life and who you are allowing to *Contaminate* your life.

▲*Make a list of the people with whom you spend the most time.*

▲*Create two columns, one labeled Contributing and one labeled Contaminating.*

▲*In the Contributing list, include the people you feel are mostly contributing to your life.*

▲*In the Contaminating list, include the people you feel are mostly contaminating your life.*

▲*Looking at your list, take a moment to realize that you are choosing to have all of these people in your life. You are at choice to shift how much time you allow anyone in your life.*

▲*Actualize a higher perspective: Each person we encounter gifts us the opportunity to wake up and heal emotional wounds. Allow yourself to Find the Gold in why you may be attracting the people who are "seemingly" mostly Contaminating your life: What is each of these relationships inviting you to heal?*

I AM
God's Desire Manifest

Spiritual AND Wealthy

Eight

Be Precise about What You Desire

Most people either don't have a clue about what they desire, or they've decided that what they desire is not within their reach. If you ask most people what they want to have or experience in their life, you may get a pretty short list. If, however, their list is lengthy, the list typically has broad strokes of generalities, such as "I want to travel more."

Although it is great to apply a broad-brush stroke of what you desire to the canvas of the life you want to create, you manifest a more extraordinary life when you get clear and precisely articulate what you want. "I want to travel more" then might become "I would like to travel to Africa and volunteer for one month supporting the health and well-being of chimpanzees."

**Being precise magnifies emotion, and
emotion creates the attraction.**

Imagine that you're at your favorite restaurant and that I'm your waitress and cook. When I arrive to take your order, and you say, "Just bring me something good to eat for breakfast," I will most likely go

I AM

back to what I remember you've usually ordered, which was coffee, yogurt with granola, with dry whole-wheat toast.

So, I bring you "the usual," but you're not pleased because you *really* wanted something else but weren't specific. When you are precise with what you are expecting, I can give you what you expect. This is precisely what happens when we co-create with Spirit.

Now when you ask me to bring you "something good to eat," and you clarify for me that you desire to have freshly squeezed orange juice; a Bhakti soy chai, extra spicy and hot; an omelette filled with tomatoes, onions, capers, spinach and cheddar cheese; and sourdough toast with extra butter, I am now clear with what you desire, and I can bring you what you want.

When you are ready to be more precise about what you desire, gift yourself some quiet time to expand as many details about what you want. The more precise you are, the more you will activate positive emotions like excitement and anticipation, which are necessary to manifest your desires.

When you find it difficult to be precise about what you desire, it's a good indication that you may have some self-limiting beliefs about being worthy to receive and being able to manifest your dreams.

You can set an intention to become aware of any beliefs you may have that are limiting you from being able to honestly acknowledge and manifest your heart's desire. While some of your limiting beliefs may appear quickly, others will appear over time; trust that you're intending an ongoing awareness to excavate and transform any limiting beliefs you discover along your journey.

In order for you to get precise and then align yourself to manifest your desires, it is important you investigate what you currently *believe*, *trust* in the unseen, and *let go* of anything standing in your way.

Believe		**Trust**		**Let Go!**
you are worthy and that you deserve whatever you desire.	⇨	that there is Infinite Supply and you are not taking away from anyone else's well-being.	⇨	of any limiting beliefs and what anyone else thinks about you or what you desire.

▲ Universal Wisdom

Your desires and how YOU consistently think and feel about receiving your desires are matched or exceeded for your highest good in the physical world.

▲ Spiritual AND Wealthy Practice

1. Create a list of 40 items that you desire.

Your list may include items such as emotional essences like more peace and joy in your life, physical objects like a new car, or experiences like marriage. The beauty is that you get to decide what you want; it's your life, your canvas, and your creation. What do you want your life to look like? Create your list as quickly as you can without "trying" to think. Be playful. Just do it.

2. Notice the following.

▲*How easily did you generate 40 items?*

▲*Are any of your items too general? Where can you be more precise?*

▲*How did it feel for you to generate these 40 items? Were there items that were more emotional for you than others?*

▲*Does your list contain a variety of items? Have you listed some big dreams, or are you playing it safe with only small desires?*

3. Be precise with your desires.

After you complete this list, take each individual item you listed and "telescope it out" by expanding it with more details. For example, if you listed

I AM

a new car, what make, model or color would you like? Do you desire a convertible, tinted windows or certain stereo system? Be specific.

4. Once you finish being more precise, do the following for each desire:

With your eyes closed, take a deep breath and imagine a blank pole in front of you. This pole represents your current vibration for attracting your desire. At the bottom of the pole is 0% (not ready yet), and the top is 100% (ready or currently manifesting).

Notice how ready you currently are to allow yourself to receive this manifestation. No judgment — just notice so that you can create any change in your current vibration.

Trust what you get for each item and note the percentage.

5. Once the list is complete with your assigned percentages, answer the following as you go through each item on your list.

▲*What must expand within me in order to manifest this desire, i.e. courage, trust or self-love?*

▲*Is there anything I need to let go of that is currently blocking my ability to manifest this desire?*

▲*Am I attempting to manifest this desire all by myself, or have I been guided to ask someone for help? Whom can I ask to support me in this desire?*

▲*Am I listening to my intuitive guidance and taking action?*

▲*What is the next action step I can take that will bring me closer to what I desire — and bring my desire closer to me?*

6. Starting with the desire that has the highest percentage on your list, write three things you can do in the next three days that support the manifestation of your desire.

▲*Take action!*

▲*Repeat this approach for your other listed items.*

▲*Continue to focus your positive thoughts, feelings and actions every day on the desires that have the highest percentages. Remember: The higher your percentage, the closer you are to actualizing your desire.*

7. Celebrate what you just completed.

You've just created an energetic and emotional shift that allows more Divine co-creation in the direction of your dreams because you've become precise with your heart's desires and focused positive thoughts and feelings in that direction.

I AM
Perfectly Aligned with All That I AM
in the Choices I Make

Spiritual AND Wealthy

Nine

Make Choices That Are in Alignment with Your Desires

One of my very favorite words in the world is *choice*. When we align our choices with our desires, we create freedom for ourselves. Freedom is our joyful and natural expression of the Divine essence we are. Your soul is all about the freedom to express joy through the process of transforming the invisible into the visible — what we refer to as manifestation. You are manifesting all the time through the choices you make with your thoughts, feelings and actions, not just when you consciously expect to create something you desire.

The choices you make create your life experiences. Each choice made is considered neutral in spiritual form. It is from the human perspective that we as individuals, communities and as collective nations apply meaning to the choices we and others make. We create beliefs based on learned behaviors about which choices are right or wrong, good or bad, moral or immoral, and so on. Then, judging choices as "black or white," we often condemn, criticize, approve or praise the choices we and others make.

There are a host of reasons why we make the choices we do. Although exploring and then discovering why we make certain choices can be important to shift our behaviors, knowing that we even have a choice in the first place is most important.

Although you may already know you have free will to create your life, most people do not and often feel their *lot in life* is perhaps their karmic punishment or destiny. When we don't believe we have much or any control over our lives, we are living from the victim consciousness. Collectively, most of us have been taught to react and create from this victim consciousness, where we blame God or others for our unhappiness, our lack and our limitations.

Blaming God or accepting that it is God's will for something that has happened is one of the best examples of victim consciousness I know. Misinterpreting religious teachings and doctrine has been a major source of perpetuating the illusion that man is separate from God as well as creating fear and maintaining control with the false belief that we are not responsible for what we are creating.

When we show up in life as a victim, we don't take responsibility for what we create in our life, and we give away our power to create from a higher vibration that conscious awareness and choice allow. From the lower frequency of disempowerment, we energetically create dis-ease, lack, limitation and the impulse to control others because we feel so out of control ourselves.

We always have a choice to create something new.

As we awaken to the realization that we are creative power and that we really do have free will, we then can begin to align the choices we make with our desires and choose to be responsible for our own happiness. We are always at liberty to make new choices when we discover that the choices we are currently making in our lives are not in alignment with our highest self and the creative impulses and inspirations that desire to emerge through us.

As we expand our awakening and consciously align our life choices, some of us resist the opportunity to grow and change because we fear loss of a relationship or what others may think about us. I love reminding people that they can choose to make new agreements with themselves or others, allowing them to be their most authentic self.

We benefit more from lovingly giving others the choice to grow with us or to continue their journey in their unique way without us. If we don't speak and act from our authentic self, we sabotage our Divine potential. Each choice allows your authentic self to either blossom or stagnate, and creates a ripple of creation that impacts your life as well as all those around you.

The very nature of our choices is directly related to expanding our consciousness.

While Spirit considers what you choose as neutral, each choice is considered valuable because it nourishes you along your spiritual journey, where you are invited to awaken to the *collective truth*:

You are One with everything, and you are co-creating with All That Is.

As you make choices that bring you closer to your desires, the manifestation simultaneously draws closer to you. This magnetic energy by definition expands your Divine essence, and you feel excitement, anticipation and ultimately *very alive*.

When you are not experiencing this *very alive* feeling, you are receiving the gift of contrast that your choice brings, and you can gain the clarity of what pleases you and what does not. I refer to this process as being the *spiritual detective*. As a *spiritual detective*, you evaluate your choices and decide whether you want to make new choices in order to be in alignment with all that you desire.

The rate of your soul growth is directly proportional to the choices that align with your desires and allow you to feel more peace, happiness, joy and contentment. *You cannot not grow*; however, aligning your choices with your desires feeds and significantly expands your joyful soul.

▲ **Universal Wisdom**

There is no freedom in seeking outside approval for the choices you make. Freedom and joy come to you as you utilize the wisdom gained from the choices you have made in the past to then create your future.

▲ **Spiritual AND Wealthy Practice**

Consider the following for aligning your choices with your desires.

1. Base your decisions from a place of where you want to be, not where you are.

▲*Is the choice I am about to make taking me closer to where I want to be, or am I delaying my good?*

2. Choose to make new agreements with yourself or others by reviewing any choices you have made in the past that aren't working for you now.

▲*Are there any areas in my life where I feel some regret in a choice that I made, where I can now choose to make a new agreement with myself or someone else?*

3. Honor yourself by choosing what you know is right and true for you.

▲*Will the choice I am about to make betray any gut feeling or inner knowing that I have or have had in the past?*

4. Embrace the opportunity to grow and change as you expand your awakening and consciously align your life choices. Gift others the freedom to choose their own growth experiences.

▲*Am I attempting to please other people with the choices I am making because deep down I am afraid they will leave me or reject me in some way?*

5. Notice whether you are owning the choices you make and the subsequent results of your choices.

▲*Am I blaming God and others for my unhappiness?*

▲*Am I making others responsible for my happiness?*

Utilize the following I AM statement often to bring you into alignment with the ability to create your own joyful experiences and manifest your desires:

> **"I AM responsible for my own happiness and well-being through the aligned choices that I make."**

I AM
Radiant Health

Spiritual AND Wealthy

Ten

Listen to Your Body's Wisdom

Imbalance in your life can create dis-ease and attract injury. Our body attempts to get our attention through illness and injury as a way to remind us to create a balanced and more joyful life. Your body actually speaks to you regularly. Depending on how well you listen, it may begin as a whisper, like having a sore throat, but possibly get as loud as a roar, like being diagnosed with cancer.

You will get out of balance by not speaking your truth, not listening to your intuition, disempowering yourself through the words that you speak, not pursuing your dreams, and engaging in anything you believe is not good for you. Personally, I know these practices of imbalance have created havoc in my own body, including chronic sinus infections, cancer and a once "incurable" autoimmune dis-ease.

Most people don't really think about why they might be experiencing dis-ease when their initial symptoms of un-wellness are subtle or their injuries are minor. Often it is not until the symptoms or injuries become chronic, serious or life threatening that people can begin to see these experiences as an invitation to assess their lives.

Unfortunately, most people don't take the time to inquire what the underlying reasons might be for their dis-ease or injury. As a society we have been trained to get medical support that typically reduces symptoms, alleviates pain, kills bacteria, and so on, but does not address the underlying cause and effect of why we are sick or injured in the first place. Both are important.

We may say that the cause, the why, of a certain ailment is a bacterial infection. Unfortunately, this diagnosis does not explain the deeper, underlying river of information our body has for us. Not only can our body tell us why we got sick in the first place, but it can also tell us how to stay more balanced in our health and even create healing where medical science says there may be no cure. Currently we have countless cases of people who no longer have evidence of dis-eases once considered incurable, such as AIDS.

**Although a diagnosis may be incurable,
symptoms and dis-ease are not.**

The intuitive guidance that came to me after my own "incurable" diagnosis was the following realization:

**"If my body could get into this mess,
then my body could also get out."**

We often *accept* that our current condition is because of our family history, and even if we haven't manifested a genetic disorder, we often *expect* to get it. I've also heard my clients chalk it up to bad luck or karma, rather than utilizing the dis-ease or injury as an opportunity to go within and create a deeper spiritual connection. We gain insight and meaning when we evaluate the areas in our life where we are not creating and experiencing radiant health.

What if dis-ease is an invitation to wake up to a better life? What if the injury is reminding you to slow down and assess what is really important to you? The gold we can find when we are willing to investigate, be vulnerable and ask meaningful questions is priceless.

**It can be life changing when we listen to the wisdom our
bodies are offering and take action on what we discover.**

Awakening to a higher perspective about what your body experience is offering can dramatically change the outcome of any dis-ease or injury, as well as reveal to you that a better life, a more joyful life, a more prosperous life is waiting for you. This higher perspective can even support you to accept, be at peace with and trust the journey of others who may be suffering with a dis-ease or injury.

Anytime you can gain clarity and higher meaning, you allow more inner peace and more prosperity.

Often dis-ease reveals itself because somewhere along the way subconscious decisions are made not to live. I have a process that helps support my clients to see and measure the degree of subconscious decisions they may have made, so they can understand the results they are currently experiencing as well as make a conscious choice to fully live.

On my own path to conscious wellness, through investigating my body's wisdom, I needed to acknowledge that I had opted out of fully living. I was making subconscious decisions to slowly die. I learned that dis-ease and injury are our opportunities to opt back into living 100%.

I once worked with a woman who was diagnosed with breast cancer and had decided to have surgery, radiation and chemo. After she finished her treatment choices, I had the intuitive hit during our session that she had made a subconscious decision not to live and had not corrected this choice to fully live. As we worked together, she was able to realize that she was only 75% committed to staying on the planet at that time. From this discovery, she could then make a conscious choice to *truly live* rather than just *exist in a less-than-vibrant life* that would continue to yield unfavorable experiences.

When your spirit is saying yes to this journey, but subconsciously your personality or *egoic* self is saying no, you will experience dis-ease or injury. You might think, "Not me, I would never say that or feel that." Surprisingly, I didn't think so either, but there was a time when I felt life was hard and that it would be easier and less painful to just leave the planet. Thankfully, the love for my children initially inspired me to investigate any dis-ease, excavate my soul and begin to see life as a beautiful, miraculous and amazing gift.

When we see life as a beautiful, miraculous and amazing gift, we allow ourselves the time to enjoy our lives. As a society we often don't value leisure time enough to schedule rest, rejuvenation and play. Most modern societies value being busy over allowing time to reflect, relax and connect. Our days are often packed with so many things to do and places to be, *which often are things we really don't even want to do*.

Illness and injury are generally acceptable ways and excuses to take a break (brake) from our responsibilities. They're also acceptable ways to get attention and loving support. When we're not feeling loved or worthy of love, or when we need a "break" from our busy lives, we may subconsciously create dis-ease or injury so that we can get the attention and support we desire but we're currently not able to ask for. Ouch, right?

Interestingly, notice how often you or others have said, "I need a break," when you felt overwhelmed or frustrated. Consistently repeating, "I need a break" may result in an actual broken bone or some form of un-wellness that slows you down, like the flu. If you consciously acknowledge and take action to create more space for rest or time away from a stressful environment, your body won't need to get your attention through dis-ease or injury.

Your body will reveal a wealth of information for you, when you choose to listen. Trusting your intuition and taking responsibility for your own health and well-being take practice, intention and curiosity.

▲ Universal Wisdom

Love consistently and creatively calls forth for the Divine recognition of the individualized self to consciously return to the whole and claim the Divine perfection that IS.

▲ Spiritual AND Wealthy Practice

When you're experiencing illness or have some sort of injury—even subtle aches or pains, you can use the following steps to bring your life into alignment and create greater health.

1. Set an intention to connect with the illness or injury by *temporarily focusing* **on the part or parts of your body that are symptomatic.**

2. Close your eyes and see the energy of the illness/injury by noticing what it looks like as far as *shape, size, color* **and** *texture.*

3. As you feel more connected to the possibility of gaining Divine wisdom from the illness or injury in your body, ask the following questions.

▲*Why do you want my attention?*

▲*Is there anything I need to do so that I can return to my natural state of health and well-being?*

▲*Is there anything I need to stop doing so that I can return to my natural state of health and well-being?*

▲*What must I let go of to create an energetic shift to return to perfect health and well-being?*

▲*Is there anything that I need to know for my highest good to bring my life into alignment and create greater health?*

4. Be responsible for understanding the answers given.

If any of your answers to these questions in Step #3 aren't clear, ask Spirit for greater clarity, just as you would talk to a friend or loved one. Here are some examples for inspiration; feel free to create your own.

▲ *"Spirit, what did you mean by _____?"*

▲ *"Spirit, could you tell me more about _____?"*

▲ *"Spirit, what else do I need to know about _____?"*

▲ *"Spirit, I understand I need to let go of _____. Could you tell me how?"*

I AM

I AM
ONE with All That Is

Spiritual AND Wealthy

Eleven

Let Go of Unforgiveness

One of the most damaging energies that can negatively affect multiple areas of your life is unforgiveness. Carrying the weight of unforgiveness can create pain, stagnation and energetic blocks in every area of your life, including the energy of money and your financial freedom.

When I opened my intuitive coaching practice, I was surprised to note how many people came to me to increase their financial flow, and the most common thread that these people shared was the presence of unforgiveness.

You create pain and suffering within your emotional, mental and physical body as you *egoically* separate yourself from who you are and All That Is connected to you with thoughts of unforgiveness and wrongdoing. Because you are a Divine aspect of Spirit, when you carry the energy of unforgiveness, you amplify the illusion that you're separate from All That Is.

I invite my clients to see the beauty of excavating and evaluating why their lack of money or lack in any area of their life is an opportunity to heal wounds of unforgiveness. As they let go of unforgiveness, they begin to realign their consciousness with Divine

Mind, creating new opportunities to be in the flow of prosperity and abundance.

**Where you see and feel wrongdoing,
Divine Mind sees opportunity to restore Wholeness.**

When you hold the energy of unforgiveness, you are interfering with the energetic ability to attract what you are wanting. You are also perpetuating an energetic field from within you that continues to attract more of the same painful experiences. These experiences reflect your unforgiveness as well as the original wound that attracted the situation in the first place.

Everything you think and feel is creating an impact on the quality of what you are experiencing in your life. The negative impact of unforgiveness is the same, whether you carry unforgiveness toward yourself; others, like your friends, family or coworkers; or toward establishments, such as the government, the church or a corporation— it ALL counts.

**You must let go of unforgiveness towards
yourself in order to create a Spiritual AND
Wealthy life full of joy and freedom.**

I realize that letting go of unforgiveness can be one of the messiest, most uncomfortable and most resisted areas along your journey. *I've been there.* But here's what I know to be true: When you focus your energy around being willing to forgive and then create the internal shift through spiritual practice, you will finally free yourself to be able to create the life you've always longed for.

▲ **Universal Wisdom**

To hold the current of unforgiveness towards yourself or others magnifies the illusion of separation, creating disharmony between the individual expression and the Divine expression of your life. You are ONE with everyone and everything.

▲ Spiritual AND Wealthy Practice

1. Be willing, with an open heart, to heal any unforgiveness.

Write and answer the following questions, one at time. Write your responses as a list.

This process may be uncomfortable as you move through these questions and allow your authenticity and honesty to emerge; however, these feelings are only temporary. Ignoring any area of your life that holds unforgiveness will continue the cycle of creating more pain, lack and limitation, rather than allowing more flow in all that you desire.

Please don't concern yourself with trying to let go of unforgiveness all at once. If that happens, great, but for most people this process is an ongoing spiritual practice, and sometimes consistent baby steps are what create the avalanche of change to occur. This practice allows you to be more aware and invites you to choose to do something different.

▲*Whom am I holding unforgiveness towards? List as many people who come to mind.*

▲*What am I holding unforgiveness towards? List as many situations that come to mind.*

▲*Are the areas where I am holding unforgiveness contaminating any other areas of my life? If so, what areas come to mind?*

▲*Are the areas where I am holding unforgiveness contributing to any other areas of my life? If so, what areas come to mind?*

2. Be willing to investigate how willing your current energy is to let go of unforgiveness and forgive.

On a scale of 1 through 10, honestly and without judgment, rate your current level of willingness to forgive with each item that you listed in #1, using the following guidelines.

One (1) represents an area where you feel the least resistance to forgive, and 10 represents where you feel the most resistance to forgive. Note that where you have the greater the resistance, you also have the greater growth opportunity, which is discussed in the "Embrace and Celebrate Resistance" chapter.

3. Be willing to forgive.

▲*Now choose the lowest-numbered item from your list. If you have multiple items with the same low number, choose all of these items.*

While you may want to tackle the biggest challenge or opportunity by looking at the item where you feel the most resistance, you can often feel even more accomplished if you choose the area with the least resistance. One of my mother's suggestions has always been to "clean the room with the least number of things to do, so you can have more of a sense of accomplishment and completion."

▲*Now write the following:*

I AM now willing to let go of any energy of unforgiveness that I have carried, and I now open to receive the clarity, freedom and joy that forgiveness brings. I choose to take this step, starting with _____ [fill in the blank with your lowest-numbered item(s)].

▲*Sign with your full name and date this declaration. By declaring this statement, you will be intuitively guided to allow this forgiveness process to unravel in a gentle way that is right for you.*

▲*As you move forward, pay attention to any ideas that inspire and nudge you to let go of any feelings of unforgiveness.*

▲*Take action on any nudges and inspirations you receive, without delay.*

4. Take your forgiveness practice to a higher vibration.

Keep going!

Practice forgiveness from a higher level: Complete #2 of the Spiritual AND Wealthy Practice in the "Feel Your Magnificence" chapter, if you haven't already.

I AM
the Pure Thought of Divine Mind

Spiritual AND Wealthy

Twelve

Detoxify Your Brain

Some of us have grown up with the saying, "A mind is a terrible thing to waste." This phrase was coined during a campaign slogan in the early 1970s by the United Negro College Fund to inspire African American students to seek higher education above other distractions that could waste the potential of a promising student.

This campaign's primary purpose was to educate this audience about one of the biggest distractions at that time, the use of drugs. This message has expanded beyond this particular demographic and the distraction of drug use to apply to *any* sabotaging behaviors we have created individually and collectively. "A mind is a terrible thing to waste" now invites our subconscious mind to move beyond *any* distraction and persevere forward.

When we are evolving the essence of what being Spiritual AND Wealthy really means, we are speaking the same language about disallowing anything to distract us from our creative potential in any endeavor.

Abusing drugs is a great example of how people distract themselves and create a toxic lifestyle. Unfortunately, the most overlooked drug of choice, which is completely legal, is *negative thinking and worrying*. Our thoughts create chemical reactions in our body, just like any other drug, and the effects can be just as devastating to us in the long run.

The drug of choice here is negative thinking and chronic worry. Every day through our habits and subconscious patterning, this drug is bought, sold and taken over and over again. It is completely legal but devastating and polluting our world, as with all addictions. Until we realize and change our addictive patterns of negative thinking and worrying, we too are wasting the promise and potential of our own soul's adventure.

We were not born thinking negatively or worrying;
we learned this habit, and what we learn can be unlearned.

Most of the world has been trained to focus on fear and negativity through sharing personal stories and the news, especially in the form of media. When we habitually ingest the repetitive negative format of the media, we can receive an unhealthy dose of skewed, imbalanced information that doesn't represent the reality of the overwhelming goodness that abounds here on earth. Choosing a consistent stream of negativity is like choosing to be hooked up to an IV with toxic fluid — you can contaminate multiple areas of your life.

Most of us have grown up with family and friends who were constantly reinforcing the negative news with how dangerous and hard it is *out there* in the *real world*. Because we loved and trusted these people, we bought into the focus on negativity.

Each and every time we give any of our attention to negativity and worry, we put our health at risk, we sabotage our precious relationships, and we delay future relationships, meaningful work and financial freedom. Ultimately, with worry and negativity, we are settling for "what is" rather than the higher vibration of what desires to emerge as our Divine potential.

As with any drug, negativity and worry release an onslaught of chemicals that compromise the perfection of our immune system. Chronic negative energy gets stored in various areas of our body, creating dis-ease. I tell my clients, "Imagine having a barrel of toxic waste, and every time you allow your focus to be on negativity and fear, you are taking a ladle full of this toxic waste and ingesting it."

Gross, right? No one in his or her *right mind* would do that, which is exactly the point. If you could actually see how damaging this is to your body and your life, you'd stop straight away.

To live our highest potential and explore all possibilities, we need to allow the *right mind, our Divine Mind,* to guide us to *focus on what is right with us, what is right with others and what is right with the world.* In order to open up to your soul's unlimited potential, you are responsible to become aware of the impact you have on yourself and the world around you.

Through the *Law of Attraction* or the *Principle of Cause and Effect,* we create more of whatever we focus on the most. The more you worry and negatively focus your attention, the more your experiences will reflect your focus, resulting in a negative *self-fulfilling prophecy.*

In order to shift any negative results in our life, we need to first notice, without blame or judgment, where we are subconsciously focusing our negative thought patterns. Our Spiritual AND Wealthy invitation is to become aware of our thoughts and then take action to shift any focus on negativity and worry to detoxify our mind and body.

You may want to look at everything you can think of that may be perpetuating any habits of negativity and worry you may have. Once you notice your unhealthy habits, commit to taking action to decrease them and eventually remove them by reframing your focus with more positive thoughts, words and actions.

▲ Universal Wisdom

Suffering is man-made; alignment is God's glory. As you align your vision and heart with Divine mind, that which is not you loses focus, and that which is you becomes crystal clear.

I AM

▲ Spiritual AND Wealthy Practice

1. Enjoy a 30-day detox from news, radio, television or movies that have a negative focus or agenda.

I can already hear some of you freaking out. "How will I know what is happening in the world then?" Believe me, you will know what would be relevant or important when it is necessary because you will have friends and family who will be more than eager to keep you informed.

Years before the September 11 experience, my family had made a conscious decision to not watch television in our home, yet I still heard news of this event through friends who called me straight away to let me know what was happening.

Get the television out of the bedroom! Let me offer three things to do in your bedroom instead of watching TV: Sleep, make love, read inspirational and uplifting books. Then, listen to music that promotes these three.

2. Speak only positively about yourself and what you desire.

If you are consistently putting yourself down, you will find that you will attract people and experiences that will perpetuate and prove to you that whatever you are saying must be true, but it is not the truth. It's your responsibility to take action to create new outcomes by noticing negative self-talk and replacing it with something better; even if you don't believe it's true at first, act as if it is, and so it will become.

Speaking positively is a major contributing factor to creating your Spiritual AND Wealthy life. Notice what you communicate to yourself and others; your words are powerful.

3. When you find yourself obsessing negatively in any direction, be willing to transmute these thoughts.

You can begin to shift any obsessive and negative thoughts or images by choosing to physically or symbolically transmute the negative energy you're creating.

Choose one of the following:

▲You may physically transmute these thoughts or images by writing them on paper and burning the paper,

OR

▲You may symbolically transform these thoughts or images by by envisioning them either surrounded by or placed into a Violet Flame.

Notice any positive imagery, thoughts and feelings during this Spiritual AND Wealthy practice that offer you relief. Your intention to let go allows these obsessive and negative thoughts or images to be transmuted into higher frequencies.

I AM

I AM
Magnificent

Spiritual AND Wealthy

Thirteen

Feel Your Magnificence

Extraordinary healing along our spiritual journey occurs as we realize we are not separate beings but that we are part of the entirety of everything that *is*. I humbly define *is* as everything that *has been, is now* and *ever will be*. In human terms this definition doesn't even scratch the surface of what cannot be described from our limited perspective. *You are* Divine Intelligence *and* Divine Beauty in all its forms, seamlessly connected to everything and ever expanding.

We are taught to identify who we are with our body, or what I often call our *earth suit*. As we initially become aware we are not our body, we begin to heal our perception and belief that we are neither separate beings nor the judgments we or others reflect about our body. Even as our awareness and consciousness expands with this idea, separation is often still not an easy perception or belief to let go.

Because you and I have grown used to identifying that we are our body, we have allowed ourselves to become wounded from what society, family, friends and even strangers have judged and declared what is right or true about us and for us.

I have yet to meet anyone who has not been judged negatively by someone and impacted adversely at some level. Many of us have been allowing someone else's judgment of what beauty is to be our mirror—

our reflection—of who we are. As we allow these judgments to become a false part of us, we create a distorted sense of self, which masks our true magnificent glory.

Magnificent beauty is not gender specific; it applies to all of us and literally applies to the ALL. Most people will live their entire life not ever seeing or feeling their magnificence, or true beauty. Instead, they accept what the collective culture of their time decides for them.

Each culture, as well as each time period, in human history has defined beauty with such vast differences that no one would ever be able to keep up with worldwide trends, perceptions and beliefs about beauty.

I had a huge awakening about beauty when I traveled to a private island in Fiji for one of those *mile-marker birthdays*. Before my trip I used my upcoming big birthday to inspire me to get in better shape. I wish I could tell you that my intention was pure health, which was in the mix, but my main purpose was being able to look in the mirror and *feel good about how I looked.*

Fast-forward to my Fiji birthday celebration: I had lost a few pounds and really toned my body, and I felt that I looked good. My holiday consisted of complete relaxation, pampering and food. Family-style breakfast and dinner were offered for the few guests on the island, while lunch was ordered for each couple to be enjoyed privately in some remote area on the island.

I started to notice that some of the favorite things I ordered to eat were being doubled and even tripled in our picnic basket. What should have been food for two turned into enough food for a family. It took me a few days to catch on to this gradual shift. I was feeling wasteful because there was so much food that we could not eat it all.

When I asked about our over-abundance of food, I was a bit shocked from the response I received from the women who were assigned to take care of our needs. I was told that I needed to *eat more* and that I was *too skinny*. The look on their faces could only be interpreted as feeling sorry for my *condition*. What a contrast to the compliments I had received at home and the joy I felt about how I looked!

While I was aware of the contrast of how people define beauty through art history and cultural trends, that day was a true eye-opener. Beauty on this island was about being full-figured and curvier. Wealth, its own form of beauty, in Fiji was seen as the ability to both have and consume the abundance of food to allow for those curves to take shape.

The most beautiful men and women are the ones
who *consistently connect and listen* to Spirit,
allowing them to exude confidence in their soul's beauty
and allowing their magnificence to shine through.

It is important for each of us to decide what "beautiful" means to us individually beyond our clothing size and what the ever-changing fashion industry and society deems beautiful. Even as we decide what beauty is to us and begin to heal our perceptions, if we continue to equate what we see in the mirror with who we really are, we will continue to experience the illusion that we are not enough.

We cannot see our true beautiful magnificence in any mirror.

Who we are is not what we see in the mirror or the results of how we decorate our *earth suit*. Although we have complete free will to do whatever we would like to adorn our *earth suit*—trendy fashion, jewelry, fragrance or hairstyle, the adornments will never completely align to truly knowing our beauty and owning our magnificence. Initially, this knowing can only come from a place of stillness within.

The ability to feel our magnificence comes from letting go of any painful experiences and unexpressed emotions when we permitted others to be the reflection of who we are or how we look, which means forgiving those people we allowed to hurt us with their unkind words. It also means clearly intending and expecting to have Source energy reflect to us and through us the truth of who we.

When we welcome this reflection, something extraordinary happens, what I call *a spiritual facelift*. The *spiritual facelift* is the energetic shift that happens within you, allowing your true essence to shine through from the inside out. Your *spiritual facelift* will allow others to truly see you, which can inspire them to remember their own true essence and magnificence.

▲ Universal Wisdom

You must feel your beauty; the magnificence of who you are will never be truly reflected in any mirror.

▲ Spiritual AND Wealthy Practice

Take some time to sit quietly and participate in the following guided steps.

1. Realize the impact you allow with what others think about you.

People's opinions, beliefs and judgments about us can be fickle; the Divine's reflection of us is the only constant truth. Consider the following:

▲*How often do you think about what other people think about you?*

▲*Do you assume what others are thinking about you?*

▲*Do you limit or change your actions based on your assumptions, rather than base your actions on others' actual feedback or your intuitive guidance?*

▲*Have you limited yourself by believing other people's negative opinions, beliefs and judgments about your appearance?*

2. Own your magnificence through forgiveness and forgiving.

You are invited to forgive as well as ask for forgiveness in a very neutral sense, which acknowledges your Oneness.

**As we grow more consciously through forgiveness,
what we desire for ourselves we want for others.**

With the following approach, you are invited to dissolve energetic and emotional knots that consciously or subconsciously both bind you to your past and offer keys to your freedom.

▲*Reflect on any area, from anytime in your life, when you or someone else, commented about your physical appearance in any negative way.*

▲ *Allow yourself to feel any emotions that surface, as you reflect on this time.*

In the moment of hearing or reading unkind words directed toward us, we often stuffed our authentic feelings like sadness, fear and anger in an attempt to protect ourselves; however, we also bound ourselves energetically to the illusion of separation, manifesting in our lives as unworthiness.

▲▲*Neutralize the emotional charge from this interaction by both forgiving and asking for forgiveness, even if you don't know why.*

▲▲*As you bring this person and experience to mind, forgive this person by saying the following, allowing anything that comes to mind, as if he/she were right in front of you: "I forgive you for _____."*

▲▲*Then, ask this person for forgiveness by saying the following, filling in the name of the person if you know it: "_____, please forgive me for any and all ways that I may have triggered something painful within you."*

Trust that a cause-and-effect interaction drew this experience to you, even if forgiving or requesting forgiveness doesn't make logical sense. You may feel you have not done anything to provoke this person; however, our Spiritual AND Wealthy invitation is forgiveness on all levels for the "soul" purpose of clearing any energetic bind on a higher, energetic plane, so our magnificence can shine, and we can free ourselves from any past experiences we've allowed to limit us.

Most people see forgiveness as one-dimensional; intuitively, I was shown the multi-dimensional infinity symbol, representing the entirety of forgiveness—allowing our magnificence to emerge.

When you feel any emotional charge about letting go of unforgiveness, you are still energetically bound to that person or the experience that you are allowing to hold you back.

You are always at choice to energetically free yourself.

3. Expect Spirit to reflect your magnificence.

Feeling your magnificent beauty comes from gifting yourself time to sit quietly and listen with all your senses to the energetic reflection of your Divine Beauty from Spirit, God, Source, angels and any loving, light-filled energy that resonates with you. The reason I love to connect with energy of the angelic realm is because the consistent reflection is so clear, loving and healing around any wounding we have allowed.

As you sit in stillness more often, you can create more opportunities to experience your magnificence in ongoing waves of awareness. This practice is key to truly knowing your Divine Beauty and connection to All That Is.

4. Accept the loving reflection from your brothers and sisters.

As you intend to feel your magnificence and have it reflected to you, notice that your earthly brothers and sisters will lovingly begin to reflect your Divine essence. Your invitation is to receive compliments and recognition without dismissing any and all forms of Love that are being offered to you.

Notice all the ways the Universe will reflect your magnificence to you when you are ready to listen.

The more you trust yourself and your aligned inner dialogue
with the Divine, the less frequently you will seek
other people's opinions and approval. This is freedom.

I AM
Love

Spiritual AND Wealthy

Fourteen

Find the Gold in Everything

One of my personal philosophies and practices is to "Find the Gold." *Finding the Gold* means acknowledging the gifts that come to us in *all* situations. My philosophy goes far beyond "the silver lining." This mindset actively, consciously and with 100% expectation affirms that you can find gold in ANY experience or situation you encounter.

You can even *Find the Gold* in areas you have felt were your worst experiences. Is this practice easy? Not necessarily in the beginning, but let me assure you from experience that it is *so* worth it.

When you first begin to use this practice, *Finding the Gold* can seem very far away and, in fact, can bring up feelings of anger if you are still in a situation that feels too painful. Your Spiritual AND Wealthy invitation is to be willing to give up how painful you are feeling in exchange for feeling better. Surprisingly, not everyone *consciously* desires to feel better.

This practice honors that these experiences are worthy of exploration. It honors any reactions and emotions you have experienced. It also honors any emotions that you may need to feel and process, so you can move through to the other side of them. I like to remind my clients that it's okay to visit anything uncomfortable and process as necessary, but we don't want to live there.

This practice can really speak to the events that are the most challenging for you; the ones that you may feel you can't overcome. *Find the Gold* so that you can forgive, let go and be free.

Can you imagine speaking about the most painful event in your life and not experiencing pain around it? Seeing the experience from a *higher perspective* frees you from the pain and is the gift in *Finding the Gold*.

Staying stuck or devastated does not allow for the exponential growth and expansion of your soul — *Finding the Gold* does.

When you are willing and expect to see any situation from a higher perspective, you will be shown information that can give you freedom from any painful experience. As *Finding the Gold* becomes your natural practice, life becomes easier and more rewarding for you.

I have had many opportunities in my own life to *Find the Gold*. At one time, someone very close to me unknowingly ingested a cookie that contained medical marijuana. This person was very young and had never experienced any mind-altering drugs before, and the effects frightened me.

This experience triggered several painful reactions for everyone involved, including anger, frustration, mistrust, confusion, sadness and judgment. As I processed and honored all the feelings that came up for me, I had the opportunity to ask myself as well as the people involved why they felt they attracted this situation into their lives. For me, this was one way to *Find the Gold*.

As you open up more to *Finding the Gold* in challenging situations, it's great to ask, "Why have I attracted this situation into my life?" When I asked Spirit why I attracted this particular situation into my life, I was given two words: *compassion* and *forgiveness*. Initially, I admit that I shook my head and rolled my eyes because I was experiencing feelings of anger and sadness. I knew these words to be the truth I needed to hear, yet, in order to *Find the Gold*, I needed to have some conversations with everyone involved so that I could *expand the energies within me* of both compassion and forgiveness.

But I wasn't done processing to *Find the Gold*. I also needed to cry and grieve for the innocence I felt was lost. As I further explored *Finding the Gold*, I was intuitively shown the reason I attracted this experience—the unhealed wounds that were triggered in me from growing up in a family who not only used illegal drugs but also sold them and my own innocence lost.

Finding the Gold for me took *being willing to* listen intuitively, be authentic, and hold forgiveness and compassion in my heart, even though in the beginning it wasn't easy to do.

The places we can find the most gold are those places in which we also find initially the most difficult to do so.

Without looking for the gold, the choice to stay in anger and all the other lower energies would have created ongoing shame, unforgiveness, separation and blame. It would not have allowed me to see the *higher truth* being revealed and what wanted to be healed.

The result was that all of us became closer. We found gold in the tears and the opportunity to heal wounds that were more than 15 years old. Eventually, we experienced the relief and freedom in the form of laughter, hugs and kisses.

Living from this space, this practice allows you to feel better and even more joyful than without it. It can improve your health by not staying stuck in negative feelings that stress your body and compromise your immune system. It expands your consciousness and allows you to see beyond the perspective of our *egoic* experiences so that you can see and feel the grander essence of your very being.

In this experience with my loved ones, my soul desired to experience itself as forgiveness and compassion. I had an opportunity to *choose* these experiences through the practice of *Finding the Gold*. You can *Find the Gold* in any area of your life by asking what your soul needs to experience and accepting that the answers you receive may not be what you expected, but what you need to heal and expand your soul's essence.

▲ Universal Wisdom

Everything is orchestrated for your behalf. There is not anything that does not contain in its demonstration a collective call home to who and what you are.

▲ Spiritual AND Wealthy Practice

1. Consider a current or a past situation that needs higher understanding and healing.

Then, ask yourself the following high-vibrating, clarifying and revealing questions and note your answers.

▲*What way of being do I need to let go of to see this situation or person from a higher perspective?*

▲*In what ways am I being asked to grow and expand my consciousness?*

▲*What would be a more meaningful way to see what I have attracted into my life experience from a higher perspective?*

▲*Is there anything I need to know for my highest good about this situation or person?*

2. Don't ever settle for chronically feeling miserable, angry, resentful or hurt.

The most loving choice for self-care is to rapidly move lower frequencies out of the mind and body, rather than allow the toxic thoughts and feelings associated with them to poison you.

3. Create expectancy within yourself by intending to *Find the Gold*.

Simply adopt this idea as your own philosophy and expect that in every situation there is gold to be discovered. This practice activates a high vibration that will support a healing perspective and understanding.

I AM
Living Gratitude

Spiritual AND Wealthy

Fifteen

Be Present in the Grace of Gratitude

We have a propensity to focus on our past and our imagined future without being *right here, right now.* The only place we can continue our journey is from where we are right now.

There is value in reviewing your life to learn, heal or bring forth joyful memories. Your Spiritual AND Wealthy invitation is to free yourself from regret and wishful thinking about your past. It's also valuable to envision your future with excitement and anticipation. However, your Spiritual AND Wealthy invitation here is to free yourself of any worry, anxiety and fears about the future, lest you actualize them.

Gratitude is the practice that brings you *right here, right now.* Gratitude can dissolve the regrets of yesterday and the worry of tomorrow by bringing you continually into the present moment, where you are creating your future experiences through your thoughts and emotions.

You create *more to be grateful for* when you focus your attention on being grateful with what you have right now.

One morning I woke up with pain in my right arm and shoulder. I initially thought that I slept on my arm awkwardly and assumed it would resolve itself. As the day went on, it was clear that the pain wasn't going away. The pain continually attracted my focus, and I felt distracted and worried that I had manifested a previous immune disorder. I was intuitively guided to seek answers within.

When something shows up in my physical body or as an outer experience that I don't understand or enjoy, the best practice I have learned is to ask Spirit questions. On this particular day I asked, "What is it I need to know about this situation?" The one-word answer I received on that particular day was *gratitude*. It felt like *an invitation* to be grateful, which seems illogical when one is in pain. I am always amazed with the directions and answers I receive when I consciously connect with Source energy.

My logical mind was initially surprised by the answer, yet my heart was not surprised at all. So, I sat and streamed within my mind all the things that I was grateful for in my life. When I had a moment where I couldn't think of anything else, I asked Spirit to show me more things, experiences as well as people that I could be grateful for until I felt complete.

I began to notice that I no longer could feel the pain in my arm and shoulder. I became so present in and with the practice of being grateful that I did not experience the pain in my arm, thus *the grace of gratitude.*

This practice helped me realize that I had been subconsciously directing my attention and energy to things that felt painful and did not please me, which was literally creating pain. The pain was my body's wise way to support me to realign my focus and energy with the Source that I AM.

Although the pain did not completely go away, it dissipated as my focus shifted with gratitude. Clearly, I needed the lingering effects; otherwise, without this pain, I probably would have returned to my negative focus and not embraced the *grace of gratitude*.

Pain is not a punishment; it's your
soul's request to pay attention.

When you are ready to be free of pain and long-term suffering, your Spiritual AND Wealthy invitation is to include the practice of gratitude *now*—don't wait for that *someday* to be grateful for that *something* that you finally manifested. This practice will propel you beyond the victim consciousness and into the freedom and power of creating the life you desire and is key to a Spiritual AND Wealthy mindset and life.

Gratitude includes acknowledging *all* the events, people and experiences you deem positive and wonderful; it also includes *all* the events, people and experiences that you have, *until now*, felt were difficult and painful.

Why do I say *up until now?* Because my practice and the guidance I have been given from Spirit assures me that *it all counts*. All of our experiences have served each and every one of us to be exactly who we are right in this moment. All experiences have offered us opportunities to awaken, so they are all good, despite our individual judgments about them. Your invitation from this moment forward is to take the opportunity to see things differently. You are being reminded that you have the choice to change your mind—thoughts and feelings—about anything or anyone.

All of our experiences provide us with degrees of contrast. Contrast allows us appreciation for what we want and what we don't. In each and every moment, we are invited to make new choices or continue doing things the same way.

In practicing the grace of gratitude, you can lift yourself, your energy, your perspective and your deeper understanding to move you through a difficult or painful event, allowing you to appreciate the gifts from any type of experience.

Even when you may feel it's impossible to move on from a painful experience, you can heal with the *grace of gratitude*. Let's say, for example, you have experienced someone being dishonest with you. Perhaps you felt betrayed and hurt. Maybe you lost your trust in this person.

Having been the betrayer and the betrayed, I've now learned to see this situation from a higher perspective. My inner conversation now sounds like this: "I am grateful for this experience because it has shown me how it feels to mistrust someone, feel betrayed by someone and lose my faith in someone."

Additionally, I can go further with processing in gratitude: "I can be grateful for my own understanding from this experience because I don't want to be a person that others don't trust. I don't want to be a person that someone feels betrayed by. I don't want to be a person that someone loses his or her faith in."

From this experience with dishonesty, I can choose to be more conscious with speaking truthfully to all the people I encounter. Then, I know I have shown up in a way that I expect to be treated. When I am authentic with my word, I am in alignment with my highest self and will attract more experiences with people speaking authentically to me and fewer experiences with people speaking dishonestly.

It's easier to be thankful for what we call our positive experiences, right? I chose a "negative" experience as my example because this is where we *Find the Gold* and heal.

The spiritual practice of being present in the grace of gratitude includes all of our experiences — what we deem positive as well as negative.

Your *daily* practice is to be self-aware throughout your day of all the things, people and experiences that invite you to a higher perspective. This practice establishes a new pattern within you to begin to see the good in everything. Then, you can get unstuck from negative thinking and habits that keep you from having an expanded, joyful life.

▲ **Universal Wisdom**

Gratitude begets more gratitude.

▲ Spiritual AND Wealthy Practice

Designate a personal notebook or journal to record your daily sources of appreciation at the end of each day. For the next 40 consecutive evenings, complete the following three steps.

1. Shine the light of gratitude on the past.

Consider any past experience, even from today, that felt uncomfortable. A situation may come into your awareness that is unresolved and is now ready to heal. Ask Spirit to show you some way to see this from a higher perspective. In your journal, write any wisdom, ideas or inspiration that you receive.

2. Feel the presence of gratitude every day.

Write the name of one person or experience that you feel grateful for today. Next, close your eyes briefly and receive a breath; feel the expansion of your heart as you think about this moment or person.

3. Summon the future with gratitude.

Write one desire that you would like to manifest. Using all your senses, imagine you have already achieved your desire and answer the following. What are the associated images, feelings, fragrances, tastes and sounds that you associate with this desired manifestation?

Answer the following with as much detail as possible in your journal.

What does it look like?
What does it feel like?
What does it smell like?
What does it taste like?
What does it sound like?

I AM
Divine Celebration

Spiritual AND Wealthy

Sixteen

Become a Lover of Life and Celebrate Every Day

Celebration is one of the most overlooked Essential Keys to creating both a Spiritual AND Wealthy life. It also can be one of the most fun additions to your spiritual practice. How you celebrate can be as elaborate as you like, but in order to create more of the wonderful things you desire, your Spiritual AND Wealthy invitation is to celebrate more than just the *big moments and goals* in life. Start celebrating even the things you may deem "challenges" as well as simple joys you may often overlook.

Typically, most people choose a goal, something they desire to experience and attract into their life, and go after it. When they achieve it, they often move on to the next goal after minimal or no celebration.

True celebration is more than just achieving the goal: When we truly celebrate, we acknowledge anything that transpired along the way to manifesting our desired outcome, including meeting and overcoming our fears and resistance. Everything then becomes worthy of celebration. When we consistently appreciate our own transformation and the people, places and things that unite to co-create with us, *even when it feels challenging*, celebration can become a daily practice.

I AM

You may have heard that life, overall, is about the journey and not the destination. While a great perspective, this view can imply that we should more so value the *getting there*, which leaves the actual *arrival* without much energy, sometimes creating a let-down for people.

It is vital to celebrate both the small steps along your journey as well as the arrival at each of your destinations.

The *getting there* portion of your manifestation can be full of excitement and challenging opportunities. There are opportunities for creativity and soul expansion or what we call growth. The journey is a mind, body, spirit activation that creates an intense flow of life force energy in and through us. It is the fuel for our soul to experience life at its fullest.

The *arrival* portion of your manifestation, although exciting, as well, often gets cast aside as the next new desire is *naturally* inspired within you. Because you are a creator, you will always desire something new, which is your nature and the very essence of how your soul expands. What creates more ease and grace in all of our creations is pausing long enough to celebrate all of it.

We are the essence of pure, co-creative celebratory energy.

When we step into the energy of celebration, we bring one of the highest vibrations into our very being because we are aligned with our highest self. We literally hit a high note, a perfectly tuned key or string, just as we would on a fine-tuned instrument.

Conscious celebration literally recalibrates your energetic resonance.

You raise your vibration to a state of joy and well-being, and you send an energetic ripple into the Universe. This energetic ripple says, "I really love what just happened, and not only do I love it, but I also expect more of these life experiences that allow this joyful expression through me." The Universe will mirror this request and celebrate with you. The more you focus your energy around celebration, the more experiences you will attract to celebrate.

From a higher vantage point, not only do you benefit, but others also benefit. This joyful ripple extends beyond you, touching those in your immediate vicinity and literally touching the world around you. For those of you who get stuck in feeling helpless and unsure of how you can make a difference in the world, remember that you make a difference with everything you do.

Our energetic essence cannot be contained just within our physical bodies or what I call our *earth suit*. Most people feel that *all they are* is contained within their body, yet our energy actually expands beyond and is always connected to the Universe, or what I call *Oneness*.

We can impact an entire room. Think of when you have been at a gathering, and someone walks in and is in a foul mood. You can feel it, can't you? Simultaneously, when people show up in a great mood, you can feel that energy, as well. These people can impact the entire room in a positive way. As you create a daily practice of celebration, you can also create a greater impact wherever you go.

When you want to impact the world and create ease and grace in manifesting your desires, then it's time to love and celebrate all areas of your life each and every day!

▲ Universal Wisdom

Your Divine nature is celebration. All That Is consistently celebrates you, and when you consciously match what you are with that which IS, you are in complete joyful alignment.

▲ Spiritual AND Wealthy Practice

1. Embrace moment-to-moment celebration.

Stop waiting for what you think is worthy of celebration; look for something in your current moment. For instance, celebrate the fact that you are reading this book and gifting yourself the time to reflect on and shift your Spiritual AND Wealthy consciousness.

2. Beyond this moment, start noticing how much you celebrate yourself and all you do.

You can create a daily "To Do" list and celebrate every goal you completed on your list at the end of the day.

3. Record your daily celebrations in a journal.

Before going to bed, write at least one thing to celebrate from your day. After you write it, feel how good it is to focus your attention on ending your day on a positive note.

4. Magnify your celebration with music.

I dance to a song by KC and the Sunshine Band, called "Keep It Coming Love." The song inspires me to move my body, and I imagine the words as my request to the Universe to keep the positive experiences coming my way.

5. Be creative and spontaneous with your celebration.

Do something that is different, extraordinary and FUN for you. The following are some ideas to inspire you: get a massage, go out for a yummy dinner, take a day off of work and stay in your pajamas, register for an art class, walk in nature, try a new activity with a loved one. Be silly—why not?

I AM
Ever-Expanding Love

Spiritual AND Wealthy

Seventeen

Surrender to Unconditional Love

You have chosen to expand the frequency of Unconditional Love in this lifetime. Your journey and all that is included in it is an invitation to remember the Unconditional Loving energy that you are. To surrender to Unconditional Love is to consciously do something extraordinary, and to do something extraordinary is your very nature. You may be surprised to realize that most of us in this lifetime have not actually experienced Unconditional Love—giving and receiving love without any attachment or judgment.

Most of us have only experienced love with conditions. When we deny this truth, we perpetuate our resistance to receiving Unconditional Love. I can already hear some of you debating otherwise. Yet, when you are willing and ready to live in truth with reverence and vulnerability, you will see that the love you have been giving and receiving may not always have been Unconditional Love.

Many of us have only had glimpses of giving as well as receiving Unconditional Love. For me, that glimpse, that space, was held by my grandfather. I knew with every fiber of my being that he loved me no matter what. I was just being me, and he was just being him, fully and energetically engaged; even if he was busy working in the engine room of his boat, I would sit in the doorway and talk to him, and not once did I feel his mind and heart were anywhere else but fully present with me. I don't know that he ever held the space of Unconditional Love for anyone else. I trust that this sacred space was his gift to me to know what was possible.

Who is that person for you? Some of my clients have not been able to recall a single person who loved them no matter what they said or did. For many of these clients, that presence of Unconditional Love has actually been a beloved pet. Our animal friends invite us to experience the presence and gift of Unconditional Love every day.

It may be shocking at first to realize many of our relationships are conditional. Too often we behave in ways to please other people, or they behave in ways to please us, believing we will earn love and approval as a result. When one of us changes in any way that is not pleasing to the other, often we or the other person will pull away. This is *conditional love*.

Our Spiritual AND Wealthy invitation is to choose practices that allow us to surrender to Unconditional Love and also notice when we resist, so we can make new choices to expand our soul's journey.

All the reasons we resist Unconditional Love are conditionally based. Within the illusion that we are separate from the Collective Whole, we subconsciously feel we have been abandoned and that there must be something wrong with us. Some traditions even teach us that we were born sinning and needing forgiveness.

The belief that we are flawed and unlovable subconsciously then manifests negative experiences that match and *egoically* prove that we are flawed and unlovable. Rather than seeing this as an opportunity to heal an untruth, we view it as truth.

The wounds of feeling unlovable create our inability to truly experience Unconditional Love *until* we are aware that this negative feedback loop is all a lie. We can remember and experience that not only did we come from Love, but we are also Love through quieting our minds so that we can feel, hear, see and know the presence of Unconditional Love.

As we quiet our minds and surrender to Unconditional Love, we may feel very uncomfortable in the beginning. The vibration of Love will powerfully reveal and touch all areas of unworthiness and separation that you have allowed to live within your energetic field and physical body.

Initially, when consciously surrendering to Unconditional Love, two common experiences occur. One is that we may become very emotional. It's important to give ourselves permission to cry, in order to beautifully release sadness and long-held negative emotions. Your tears are living proof of the transmutation of dense energy, the illusion of who you *think* you are, to reveal your light-filled energy, the reality of who you really are—Divine Love.

Another experience people tend to have is what I refer to as a *spiritual orgasm*, where you can feel lovingly held in a spectrum of ways. A *spiritual orgasm* can feel like a subtle chill or tingling in parts of your body, or an enjoyable full-spectrum flood of radiating energy throughout your entire body.

You may sense a profound pressure surrounding your body, holding you in a moment of stillness and inviting you to pay attention and trust that something extraordinary is at hand. You may also feel more intensely moved to a euphoric or ecstatic state, which may feel like you have transcended your body completely. In these moments, people often glimpse and know that they are One with everything.

As we surrender to Unconditional Love and these experiences, we benefit from feelings of peace, tranquility, compassion, self-love, courage, faith and trust. We also realize our individual worthiness and uniqueness within the collective Oneness.

▲ Universal Wisdom

The degree to which you surrender to Unconditional Love is the degree to which you will experience your Infinite potential.

I AM

▲ Spiritual AND Wealthy Practice

1. Intention is everything.

Set an intention to surrender to Unconditional Love, and say,

"I AM open and willing to receive Unconditional Love."

2. Do something different.

For the next 30 days, do at least one of the following each day:

▲*Write, speak and feel I AM statements throughout your day. See the "Choose Your Words Wisely" chapter for guidance.*

▲*Do something wonderful each day for yourself or for others, without any attachment or condition.*

▲*Allow others to give to you without feeling like you need to give back in some way. Just receive.*

3. Get your meditation practice on!

People can experience Unconditional Love in a variety of ways. The most consistent and profoundly impactful way is to begin and sustain a listening practice or meditative practice. Every teacher guided to serve others in their awakening as well as further their own awakening encourages regular intervals of stillness. Allow yourself to experience a variety of different teachings to see what feels most aligned for you.

I AM
Open to Receive the Love of Spirit
in All Creative Ways

Spiritual AND Wealthy

Eighteen

Expect Money to Flow in a Multitude of Ways

We live in extraordinary times. Never in our evolutionary history has there been such a variety of innovative ways to create income as there are today, proving that we are evolutionary beings in perpetual energetic expansion. We continue to expand collectively as we increase our consciousness and accept that it is *OK* for people to have more than one career choice throughout their life.

As we witness and accept that we are not limited to just doing one thing to generate the energy of money in our direction, we begin to see and know that some people are actualizing multiple streams of income simultaneously and creating extraordinary income for themselves.

Throughout history many people have accepted that they will only have one source of income that comes to them from their *job*. Our Spiritual AND Wealthy invitation is to reframe this idea and see that, although there is some truth here, some of us have had it a bit backwards.

**Be open to receive all forms of creative cash flow
and financial freedom from the energy of Source.**

When we withdraw our energy from expecting only one way to attract money and open to trusting that Source is our source, we then allow our Co-Creative Energy with Source and our conscious connection to Source to reveal extraordinary ways for money to show up in our lives.

Rather than *trying* to figure out *how* to make money, the paradigm shift that can occur for you begins when you fully appreciate that there are unseen forces orchestrating and aligning the perfect people, places, things and situations for your highest good, especially when you are also in alignment with thinking, feeling and expecting only the highest good for yourself.

Years ago I wasn't allowing for extraordinary ways for money to flow to me. I believed success around money meant that the majority of my income had to come from my primary source of employment. I had already created multiple sources of income that had nothing to do with my job or what I was passionate about; however, I was stuck in lower energetic thinking. For a while I was blind to what Spirit was continually showing me. I was being asked to surrender to how I thought attracting money should look so that a higher version of all that was possible could reveal itself in ways I could not have imagined.

Let go of thinking that manifesting more money into your life must look a certain way.

My idea of success was that the major source of my income would come from my passionate work, rather than seeing myself as already successful with simultaneous careers and income streams. When I began to heal my stubborn thinking, I thought, "Do I really care about all the details of how I will attract my ever-increasing financial flow?" I realized that as long as *how* I was creating financial abundance was legal and joyful, I was open to any and all ways that Spirit gifted and reflected my vibrational level of my thoughts and feelings about manifesting money.

An unexpected opportunity to create more financial flow appeared when I was asked to loan investment money for a friend's business.

My lawyer advised me to think about it very carefully because on paper it looked like a huge risk. Intuitively, however, I could see that her energy around this business venture would be successful and that she would eventually have multiple locations. I was clear about what I would do based on the intuitive guidance I received.

Each person she had asked for financial support had been waiting for someone else to invest in her first, so she was feeling a bit stuck. Once I said *yes*, I knew the other investors would fall quickly into place, which is exactly what happened. I was shown that my *yes* was not just about *the money*; it was about supporting her healing by reflecting confidence in her ability to see more of her authentic reflection from Spirit through my actions.

The agreed-upon interest on the loan offered me a greater return on my investment than I was earning at my bank, so it became a win-win orchestration of Co-Creative Energy. Not only did she create her first business, but she now also manifested multiple locations!

An even more extraordinary experience occurred when she was manifesting her second location. She invited me to lunch and asked me if I would be willing to accept a generous five-figure amount of money beyond our loan agreement! Desiring to "practice what I teach," I opened myself to receive what was being offered from Source through my friend.

Each of us can create wonderful opportunities to say yes and receive more financial flow, more money, and more re-Sources to create more freedom in our lives as well as an increased ability to serve others.

▲ Universal Wisdom

Financial flow is unlimited. Any limits you experience are held within your vibration.

▲ Spiritual AND Wealthy Practice

1. Let go and let your cash flow.

Our thoughts and feelings about money can very much be a part of our awakening. Become what I call a spiritual detective by making it your priority to let go of any negative thoughts, words or habits that are contaminating your frequency and restricting your money flow.

With your commitment and intention, there are infinite ways to discover clues that are answers to why you may not be attracting money at the level that you truly desire. One great way to start is to listen to how you speak about money and how you feel about people "with money."

2. Open to your inner genius.

While meditating, ask the following question: What wants to emerge and uniquely express through me as a way to increase and attract more financial freedom?

This extraordinary question requires you to ask it repeatedly, not because Spirit can't hear you, but so you will stay focused on the expectancy and excitement of the answers that will come. This process is not about sitting just once and having everything revealed to you, although that would be lovely. For most of us, the answers are often a gentle unraveling and unveiling that come to us as we align our positive thoughts, feelings and actions with Spirit.

3. Lose the attachment and create joy-filled expectancy.

Most of us get stuck because we expect something to look a certain way. It would be like asking Co-Creative Energy to align with you to create $100 when Spirit feels your true alignment is with $1000. You may miss the signs and symbols for the $1000 and feel like your prayers and intentions went unanswered. Expect only good to show up in your life, which I call being Christmas Excited. You have your own fun phrase alive and well inside you.

▲*Close your eyes and ask, "What is my word or phrase for my joy-filled expectancy?*

4. Do what you love and run it as a business.

If you are an entrepreneur or are guided to be one, make sure you understand that what you do is a business and not a hobby. If you want a hobby, have a hobby, but if you want to create amazing income from your business, then you need to learn how to operate and market what you are passionate about by learning from someone who is successfully doing what you desire to do or are doing. Aligning your skills AND your high-vibration mindset is what will manifest the success you seek.

▲*Do you feel the vibration of your thoughts and feelings are aligned and congruent with your desires for starting or expanding your business?*

▲*Do you need to align your skills and knowledge around how to operate and market a successful business?*

5. Look beyond your paycheck for other ways you can attract the energy of money.

You may not have recognized all the ways you are already attracting money because you may have only focused your attention on one area, such as your paycheck or your business.

For 30 days, notice when the flow of money and support around money comes to you; you may want to keep a journal. For example, notice when you go to a restaurant with a friend and your friend surprises you by paying for the entire bill. This is money flowing to you in disguised form.

It all counts.

I AM
Always at Choice

Spiritual AND Wealthy

Nineteen

"So What! Now What?"

I was sharing my vision for one of my events with a dear friend and colleague. I imagined a portion of my program starting with a large-screen projection of the question "Now What?" on either side of the stage, which would intend to initiate conversation. Then, I would invite the audience to see and act from a much higher perspective, regardless of how their lives may look and feel in that moment.

As my conversation with my friend continued, I told her that I had been using the question "Now What?" as a way to invite my clients to shift from any lower vibration and perspective of victim consciousness. We both agreed that we can *all* fall into the trap of wanting someone to change or something to be different, which is actually a very powerless place to be, hence the word *victim*.

When you are stuck in this victim consciousness, you are hoping or expecting an outside circumstance or someone's behavior to change so that you will feel better.

When I notice clients hanging out in the energy of victim consciousness, I ask them to close their eyes and imagine a person or circumstance where they feel stuck or have any negative emotion. I then ask, "What if this person or circumstance never changes? Now What?"

When I ask people these questions, I am holding a space of spiritual truth, calling forth their deep inner knowing that they are responsible for their own happiness and well-being in every aspect of their life.

As I shared my vision with my friend, we both agreed on the subject of personal responsibility, and she suggested "So What!" as a replacement for one of the *Now What's* I would have projected at the event. She asked me to imagine the left side of the stage with the screen projecting "So What!" and the right side projecting "Now What?" That moment was a flash of co-creative, collaborative brilliance.

"So What!" essentially says there is and will be *stuff* that can trigger you, push you and ultimately invite you to grow, heal and expand your consciousness. What's most important for the quality of your life experience is how much personal responsibility you bring to a situation and your ability to see it through a higher perspective. With this approach, you create specific energetic frequencies with your thoughts and feelings, which are your attracting points for manifesting your future relationships and experiences.

"So What! Now What?" was thus born. This strategy is a way for me to bring some humor and *angelic-booty-kicking coaching* to those who are willing to shift their perspective, their habits and—ultimately—their life. Their focus is then in the direction of their dreams, rather than focusing continually on what is wrong and waiting for something outside of themselves to change.

"So What! Now What?" is very much like being splashed in the face with ice-cold water. *In no way does this approach indicate a lack of compassion or love.* In fact, it is demanding your attention while simultaneously inviting you to wake up so that you stop distracting yourself from your own happiness. My intention when using this phrase is to support my clients to wake themselves up from the illusion that they have no control over their life.

**We can always regain control of our lives
when we initiate new patterns with how we
react to circumstances outside ourselves.**

When you get serious and too focused on any area of your life, "So What! Now What?" is an invitation through the eyes of Love and humor that invites you to heal and bring more love, understanding and compassion to yourself and others.

▲ Universal Wisdom

The degree to which you experience pain and suffering is the distance you have separated yourself from Love with the thoughts you are thinking. It is actually impossible for you to separate to any degree from All That Is.

▲ Spiritual AND Wealthy Practice

You have an Invitation from Love. RSVP by doing the following.

1. When you are in any kind of pain or suffering, say to yourself, "So What!"

You are not your emotions or any pain or suffering that you experience. Honor that these experiences feel real, honor that you are having these experiences and grow in your goodness because of them. For additional guidance, see the "Find the Gold" chapter.

2. Then say to yourself, "Now What?"

Whatever is showing up is an invitation to love and is exactly what you need. Whether you believe this truth or not, the truth in this moment is that you are having some opportunity that, through your pain, has your complete attention. You now get to choose whether you let this opportunity limit your well-being or whether you allow it to bring forth something more than you ever imagined possible. Then, you can return your focused attention to your true state of Love and Joy!

3. Next, receive a deep breath and answer the following question.

If this person or situation never changes, what am I going to do, be and let go of in order to restore myself to a space of peace and love?

4. Without editing, trust you know innately what to *do*. *And do it!*

Often we allow our egoic thinking to edit what we know to be true. It can come in the form of pride and righteousness that we allow to override what our heart is saying we need to do to heal. Set your ego aside and take action, so you can create joy and freedom in your life.

5. If you feel you are still stuck in any area of your life, go back to the Contents page and allow a chapter to intuitively catch your attention.

▲*Read or reread this chapter.*

▲*Meditate on the Universal Wisdom within the chapter.*

▲*Complete or repeat the Spiritual AND Wealthy Practice in the chapter.*

▲*Trust and expect that there is something golden waiting for you within the chapter to support your realignment with the energy of Love that is You.*

Now go play!

I AM

I AM

You are Love in all its forms

I AM

Free to Choose
Forgiveness
Joy
Strength
Courage
Compassion
Creativity
Stillness
All That Is
Desire Manifest
Harmonious Action
The Word
Perfectly Aligned Choices
Guided by Intuition
Radiant Health
Divine Celebration
Love
Divine Royalty
Always Supported
Aligned in Divine Mind
Willing
Living Gratitude
Magnificent
Ever-Expanding Love
Worthy to Receive
Spiritual AND Wealthy

and so much more!

Deborah "Atianne" Wilson
The Intuitive Spiritual AND Wealth Coach

About the Author

Everything that has shifted, healed and transformed in Deborah "Atianne" Wilson's life has come from the foundational knowledge that *it all matters—we all matter*. From her gift of spiritual neutrality through the portal of her intuitive abilities, she was invited to change her thoughts, emotions and every area of her life.

Deborah has been exploring questions many of us have asked as we navigate and investigate this wild and often intense experience we call life. Her initial questions like "Why me?" blossomed along her 32 years of inner spiritual inquiry to reveal higher perspectives like "What wants to be revealed now?" or "How can I see this through the eyes of Love?"

Abuse, abandonment, rejection, death, divorce, dis-ease, infertility and financial fears invited Deborah to shift from a place of depression, physical pain and *egoic* misunderstanding to extraordinary places of peace, empowerment, personal responsibility, healing, joy, authenticity and Love.

As a contemporary spiritual teacher, Deborah's passion is to offer practical application for ancient spiritual wisdom. As an author, speaker and mentor of prosperous living, she has created products and services that meet people at the level that they are ready to invest in themselves, from free offerings like her weekly Spiritual AND Wealthy radio show to platinum-level coaching programs. When people are ready to make the necessary shifts to get where they need and want to be in this life, Deborah is excited and able to assist clients worldwide.

Although a native Californian, she currently lives in Boulder, Colorado, savoring motherhood, the beauty of the mountains and all the playful shenanigans that come with living a Spiritual AND Wealthy life.

Inspiration for the
Spiritual AND Wealthy Interviews

I was inspired to interview some wonderful individuals who exemplify the essence of a Spiritual AND Wealthy life. Just like you and me, these people have experienced challenges and opportunities to grow. They grace these pages by being authentic and transparent about painful areas in their lives and reveal to us that these experiences invited them, just as our own painful experiences invite us, to triumph over any adversity by shifting their beliefs, their habits and their mindset to create something more extraordinary.

They share with us what is possible through their stories and wisdom, and I am eternally grateful to each of them for loving me and you enough to say yes to being interviewed and included in this book.

Enjoy!
Deborah "Atianne" Wilson

Bonus Section:
Spiritual AND Wealthy Interviews

James Malinchak
Featured on ABC's Hit TV Show, *Secret Millionaire*
Founder, www.BigMoneySpeaker.com

After growing-up in a small Pennsylvania steel-mill town near Pittsburgh as the son of a steelworker and a housewife – multi-millionaire James Malinchak is now one of most requested highest paid motivational and business speakers and business marketing coaches in America.

Since 2001, James' strong passion for serving others has impacted hundreds of thousands by teaching his unique personal and business strategies through his corporate and college speaking, public seminars, private coaching, books and home study courses. He has dedicated his life to helping others "Achieve a Better, Richer Business and Life!"™

James conducts LIVE public seminars attended by new and beginning entrepreneurs, executives, celebrities, actors, professional athletes, professional speakers and trainers. He also is called America's #1 speaker coach for anyone wanting to get started as a motivational speaker and start a personal achievement and corporate training company and he's the behind the scenes business marketing coach for top authors, speakers, trainers and celebrities in America today.

Giving back is a big part of James' life and he has raised hundreds of thousands of dollars for various organizations and has donated thousands of dollars of his own money to help others. Especially dear to his heart is helping kids create a successful future by developing the belief in themselves that they can overcome challenges and achieve their dreams and goals.

Deborah "Atianne" Wilson's Interview with James Malinchak

▲James: Hello, hello!

▲Deborah: Mr. Malinchak!

▲James: Hey Deb, how are you?

▲Deborah: I'm good. How are you?

▲James: I'm doing great. I'm doing great, ready to rock for you.

▲Deborah: Yes, please! It's a great thing.

Thank you so much. I have to absolutely just share what a grateful heart I have. So, thank you so much for giving me this opportunity to interview you for my book. I'm really clear even with myself that I know that your time is very valuable, and time is something that we can't ever retrieve. We can always make more money and do a lot of other things, but we don't get our time back. So, I really value that, and I really thank you so much.

▲James: Oh, anything for you, Miss Deb. You know that.

▲Deborah: Oh, you're sweet me. Oh, now I have it recorded, "Anything for you, Miss Deb." I am done with this interview. Have a good day.

So sweet, so sweet. I think gratitude is a great thing to start with. So, do you want to just go ahead and just jump in? Is that okay if I ask you a question?

▲James: Yeah.

▲Deborah: Okay, great! Let's go.

So, I think what I notice in a lot of people in the world is that sometimes the most simple things are often the most powerful things that they overlook. And I think gratitude can be one of them. And, so, I was wondering how much of an effect do you think having a grateful heart, having gratitude on a daily basis, contribute to our Spiritual AND Wealthy life?

▲James: Well, it's really is one of the foundational principles that makes the world go 'round, if you think about it. And I'm just amazed at how many people don't actually think that being thankful and grateful is something that they should practice every single day, every week, every month, every year.

I was in church today. Actually, I heard something. It said, "A thankless heart creates a....

Oh, man. How did he say it?

▲**Deborah:** You know? I actually saw that on Facebook, and I thought how perfect this is because it was one of the things I wanted to talk to you about. I know what you're saying.

▲**James:** "A thankless heart creates a discouraged heart," which means — basically, the way he went on to explain it was — when you're not thankful and grateful everyday and appreciative, it starts to create a mindset and a spirit about yourself to where things in life irritate you. You get discouraged for not possibly accomplishing things. It could be the littlest things, but it does not mean like you've climbed a mountain or something.

So, to answer your question about how important is gratitude, I mean, it's like if you can only have one characteristic next to probably, or aligned I should say, was honesty, loyalty, and trust. You'd have to have appreciation, gratitude, and thankfulness, as well. It's a very simple concept.

▲**Deborah:** It is a simple concept, and yet so powerful and so overlooked for sure.

▲**James:** I was going to say I heard this a long time ago: "Those who are grateful always seem to have more to be grateful for." And those who are always whining, moaning, and complaining always have more to whine, moan, and complain about.

▲**Deborah:** Absolutely. The essence of what they call "Law of Attraction," if that's your point of contention or your point of gratefulness. I totally can see that.

And, James, in regard to gratitude, I mean it's so easy to be grateful when things are really wonderful and delicious, and life *seems* to be going well, right? I would love to hear your share about being grateful for things that maybe didn't happen or maybe didn't go the way we thought?

▲**James:** Yeah. You hit the nail on the head. Sometimes I don't believe there are any failures. There are just learning experiences if you look at it. See   it all comes back to your mindset and how you think. So, whereas someone could be having, let's say a bad or a bad week, and everything isn't going right for them, per se, and they complain about it and basically become discouraged and ungrateful, whereas, another person says, "Look at this. This is a learning experience." Is it fun? Is it something I want to go through? No, but there's got to be a message in the storm.

I heard this analogy given a long time ago by a POW (Prisoner of War) who was captured I think for about seven years. He said, "There was myself and a lot of other folks who were captured way back in the war." A lot of them, when they are captured—this is this gentleman telling the story—a lot of them would kind of be in the, "Oh my Gosh, what's going to happen?" And they would be worried and stressed out every minute, every day, every month, every year for years, right? And he said what he did was he sat in that 4x6 cell, just like they did, but he visualized great, wonderful, happy things. He couldn't wait 'til he got home to see his family, which there was no assurance he would by the way, right?

▲**Deborah:** Right.

▲**James:** But he would play his favorite golf course over and over in his mind—things that brought him joy and happiness.

And, so, fast-forward after seven or some years of being released and for many years after, those who were with him in that captured setting had a lot of challenges understandably for years and years to come. But this guy went on to write a bestselling book, go on a speaking tour for the next 25 years telling his story, getting paid very well to do it, and helping a lot of people through his message and through his story. And, so, to answer your question…when it started out, it probably didn't go his way. He probably didn't plan to be captured and put on a cell for six or seven years.

▲**Deborah:** Right.

▲**James:** Right?

▲**Deborah:** Not at all. I could imagine. No!

▲**James:** So, it didn't go his way but, however, he chose to focus his mind, his soul, his heart, and his spirit in one direction, instead of letting it be focused in another direction. Therefore, he believes that's why his outcome, when he was released, was much better than many of those who didn't choose to focus their intention the same way.

▲**Deborah:** Amazing. Obviously, fabulous.

▲**James:** What's the message in the storm? There's the question.

▲**Deborah:** The message in the storm, yes. I call that "Finding the Gold." We're definitely going to be talking about that for sure.

One of the things that I noticed, too in the world, and you're really great about this when you talk about really creating great a mindset and a really positive, wonderful life, doing what you love and doing it well and serving others when you're doing your Big Money Speaker boot camp. We talk a lot about getting help, and I notice a lot of people have this attitude like they have to do it all themselves. And we do, of course, need to put our time in to do certain things and be out in the world. We can't just sit in the lotus position, right? There are things we need to do, and I know you talk about that a lot.

But in regard to asking for help, James, I see this idea of spiritual help, perhaps through prayer or meditation. And I see this asking for our human component: our brothers, sisters, our family, and our friends in supporting us. So for your particular philosophy, as well as, obviously, you live your life, successful, happy, joyful, spiritual person, tell me how important that is as far as the practice for Spirit, in connecting with Spirit, and what that might look at for you? And then in regard to asking for help, whether that's delegating, paying someone, asking your pastor, kind of the whole ball of wax, spiritually, like talking to God, be it unseen, and then talking to our fellow man, if you will, asking for support?

▲**James:** Well, I've never met one person—male, female, younger, older, richer, poor—or maybe poorer, actually—who has accomplished anything without the help of others. And you talk to any person who consistently and constantly accomplishes things, whatever that might be, personal things, professional things, financial, or spiritual, and I, virtually, with 100% certainty, guarantee you: They will all tell you that they have had mentors, they have had colleagues, and they've had assistance from a spouse, children, business partner, spiritual teacher or whatever that may look like.

So, the reason I said before, when I joked and said "maybe poorer," because when it comes to being Spiritual AND Wealthy, I think that those who understand the importance of spiritually getting assistance but also finding mentors or people who can help you in real everyday life, those who accomplish and succeed understand that, where those who are poor don't. Those who accomplish anything understand it, and those who don't accomplish things consistently—I'm not talking about once or every now and then but consistently throughout their lives—don't understand the importance of aligning with spirit or aligning with a mentor or many mentors in different areas here on the everyday kind of working, if you will, of our lives. And that goes across the board. I mean you study any athlete or any successful businessperson, and they all tell you how many mentors they have.

I had a Mixed Martial Arts world champion, and his name is Randy Couture. I think, Deborah, this is before you start to coming to the boot camps. Randy has been in movies like *The Expendables* with Sylvester Stallone and Jason Statham and all these top actors. So, some people may know Randy from the acting, but he was a Mixed Martial Arts world champion, and he came out of retirement at age 44, I think it was after being retired for several years, and re-won the Heavy Weight Championship a few years ago.

So, I had him come as a guest to one of my Boot Camps; my Speaker Boot Camps. And I asked him on stage. I said, "Randy, you're a world champion. You're like the best there is in Mixed Martial Arts. Do you have a coach?" And he said "No." And I said, "Excuse me?" He said, "I don't have a coach, James. I got about 7 or 8 coaches: I have a fitness coach, I have a mindset coach, I have a boxing coach, I have a ju-jitsu coach, I have a weight training coach, and I have a dietician who helps me with my nutrition."

And I thought, well, here's a World Champion, a guy who came out of retirement to win it again, and he's the best in the world at what he does, and he's saying he's got seven or eight coaches. And the one thing that you would love is he always looks up and he thanks, for him, God for letting him be in that ring every time he goes in there.

Those who succeed consistently and constantly in every area of their lives understand the importance of surrounding themselves with like-minded people and a lot of times people who are playing at a higher level. And those who don't achieve consistently in any area of their lives are the ones who think they can just go do it their own or they don't need great books like yours or they don't need coaching or mentoring like you provide or they don't need to go to seminars or so on and so on.

▲**Deborah:** Yes. Love it. And in regard to the spiritual aspect, one of the things that I have loved about working with you and watching you, whether it's on stage or having one-on-one coaching with you, is I just watch these amazing ideas and the inspirations that come through you. And I wonder if you have always felt that spiritual connection, and I wonder if, like everything else, you have put in practice to hone that type of skill, to actually hear. And could I ask you, I'm not sure what words feels most comfortable to you: God, Spirit, Source, whatever word that is comfortable to you. I'd love to hear what that word is. And do you hone that? Because I watch you—I see you—you're just this conduit of wonderful Source energy being of service in what you do. And so I wonder how is it that you honed your skill for listening?

▲**James:** That's a great question. Let me tell you this little story, and I think it will tell how I really started to hone in, tune in, connect to a higher power, if you will. For me, that higher power is God. When my sister Vicki was diagnosed, well, many years ago, over 20 years ago, with a brain tumor, doctors said she wouldn't live more than three months because one lesion in her brain turned to two and so on and so on.

She was taking so much pain medication that she was overdosing on the medication, but she had to take the pain medication because, if she didn't, the sound of the beating in her head, of the pounding of the headaches, was just overwhelming for her. So, it was sort of like, well, which one is going to overtake her: the pounding of the pain from the tumors or overdosing on the medication? It was really a bad situation.

But I had read a great book by Dr. Bernie Siegel, called *Love, Medicine & Miracles*. And, if you haven't read that book, I suggest you do. It's a phenomenal book. And it was all about the power of miracles and how people created their own or started to create with the help of a higher power, in my case – God, helped to get rid of tumors that were supposed to end people's lives.

So that's the whole part of *Love, Medicine and Miracles*. And many, many, over and over, documented cases of this book. And one of things that they talked about overwhelmingly in this book was the power of positive visualization and always believing to the last gasping breath if necessary that you are going to win and beat this thing. So, I read this book, and I became my sister's coach. This was back when I was in college.

We would do positive visualization every day. We have positive quotes and sayings all over her room. I had a note on the door that said, "If you have any negative thoughts leave them at the door because I won't let you in." I had meetings with my family and her friends that would come over. I would meet them outside and I say, "Look, I understand this is a very tough and sad situation, and you feel the need to cry, that is totally understandable, but you need to leave the room and do it outside the room. Don't do that in the room because if Vicki sees that, she's going to give up hope. And I don't care if it's to the last breath. We are not giving up hope."

So, Deborah, fast-forward, long story short, it was about three-and-half months later, and I had to go to a school in Hawaii. And so, leaving that night, knowing it was the last time I would ever see my sister alive, it was the hardest thing I've ever done in my life. But I made a deal with her before I left in her hospital room; it was about 10 to 10:30 at night, or something like that, and I had an early morning flight. And I said, "Well, I'm thinking about not going to school." And she rose up out of her bed, which is the first time she had done that in months, and she got in my face. And she said, "You go off and go to school. Don't worry about me. I'm going to be fine."

So, when I say I left that night and that was the toughest decision I have ever made, I thought that if I stayed and missed school and basically just quit school and dropped out, she would know she was dying. And I didn't want her to do that. So, leaving that night, knowing that that's last time I would see my sister alive according to medical doctors, because it was so bad, was the toughest thing I ever did, but we a made deal. My deal with her was this: even though I would be some 4,000 miles away or whatever that is, 5,000 miles away—she was in Pittsburgh, Pennsylvania, and I was in Hawaii going to school—I said, "We're going to do 50/50 and I'm going to keep fighting my 50% and you're going to keep fighting your 50%; as long as we don't quit, we're not going to lose."

So, I get to Hawaii and fast-forward. She is living over a month, almost two months, longer than she should have. Doctors have no idea how she's living. Literally, they have no idea how she is living. And, so, what I used to do every night before I would go to sleep, I would get down on my knees, and I'd look outside through the window as I was laying on my bed, and I would just talk to her. And I would look up into the sky and I say, "Don't quit, Vicki, we're winning, we're going to beat this thing. I'm not quitting and you're not quitting."

And so again, the doctors have no idea how she was living. So I was having dinner with an elderly couple. And they say, "How's your sister doing?" And I said, "You know it's just amazing." I said, "The doctors don't know how she's living, but she's not quitting. She's in lot of pain, but she's not quitting. She keeps going and keeps going." And they said something to me that made me feel really selfish. They said, "James, did you ever think that the reason she hasn't let go, and she may want to let go because she's in so much pain, but the reason she hasn't is because she doesn't want to let you down?"

And I felt really, really bad. So, Deborah, that night when I got down on my knees and I looked up that window, I said something different to her that night. I said, "Vicki we didn't lose. I know you're in a lot of pain, and you may want to just close your eyes and go off into a better place where you don't have any pain. And if you do want to do that, I want you to do that. We didn't lose because we never quit fighting. I love you, and I will see you again." And, Deborah, about four hours later, my Mom called me to tell me that Vicki passed away.

And that's when I became a huge believer in connection to people through Spirit. And answering your question, for me it's through God. People have different beliefs, but that was when I became a 100%, with certainty and without doubt, a believer, that we connect through spirit, we connect through soul, we connect through ways we'll never even understand. I mean someone like you would, but most of us average folks would never even understand.

▲**Deborah:** You're so sweet. Sometimes it's still a mystery, and I think that's how it should be. I have to tell you: I did not think in a million years that I would have tears streaming down my face in interviewing you tonight for this book.

And, again, it's back to gratitude because I've never heard that part of that story. I've heard about your sister. Even the gratitude you feel for just getting up every day and being thankful for a new day that you definitely got from an aspect of her and her life. And, yeah, I have tears. It's a beautiful story. And I just love all of it that you just shared, and I feel, "Oh my God, my heart." I'm like, "Where are my tissues? I have no tissues."

▲**James:** Well, I'm so—

▲**Deborah:** It should be right here.

And I love this idea, too, that you shared. It's like "Spirit" through other people because to me we are all Spirit. And this other couple – this older couple, actually speaking to you like one of your answered prayers in getting some knowledge that maybe you didn't have before that. And the beauty of what happened because of that. And, in truth, no one lost. It may not have turned out how everyone wanted, but no one lost. It's a beautiful. It's a beautiful story.

▲**James:** Right. And to sort of put a cap on the question you asked me awhile back before I got into that story, so, when things don't go your way, how are you still grateful? And how do still have gratitude? Well, I always think about this: I watched my sister lay there with lesions and have this pain, and never once did she ever moan, complain, or ask, "Why me?"

So, if things don't go my way, how can I have gratitude? Well, it's very simple. I always say, "I watched my sister die. She never once was upset, so what do I have to be upset with?"—Number one. And, number two, and she taught me this through just watching her, here's what I would say to myself: I don't care how tough my situation is; I know there's someone somewhere having a way more difficult time than me.

And when I think of that, and come from that place, it's very easy to be grateful even though things may not work out that way we plan. And I always just say, "Look, as long as I'm breathing and my family, friends, and people I love and care about are breathing, it isn't that bad." I mean, so what if the car doesn't start? It isn't that bad.

▲**Deborah:** Yeah. Always figure it's not starting for a reason. Maybe you weren't supposed to head out that morning, right?

▲**James:** Yeah, exactly.

▲**Deborah:** It's so beautiful. You know, your story about your sister and this idea of "Why me?" I know people who are still very stuck in losing someone them transitioning or something happening to them, something that we would definitely judge as tragic or devastating, and often people hold on to unforgiveness. They are not forgiving. Sometimes they do a blank statement to God in the "God, why did this happen to me?" Or, they are holding unforgiveness maybe towards a friend or family member or something like that. I just wonder how you see, holding on to the energy of unforgiveness, how that might affect our lives both spiritually and even from a place of—I'm going to get really specific here—but from a place of really attracting wealth. I mean wealth in the form of creating the energy of money around us and having more freedom around us to even serve others. Just how does unforgiveness resonate with you?

▲**James:** Well, the first thing is I certainly understand how someone could not forgive other folks or somebody else. I mean, I have been there. We all have been there, and if anybody tries to say, "Well, no, I have always forgiven everybody." No, not in the beginning; I guarantee we haven't.

So, first, I understand. I don't believe anybody is a bad person if they don't forgive someone. Is it the noble and manly or womanly thing to do? Yeah, absolutely, probably, but it doesn't mean you're bad if you don't. Let's just put it this way: people have been wronged, and people have been screwed over, and it's hard especially if you've helped or assisted that person in several ways, and maybe that happened to you where you felt like you were slighted. So, it's very easy to understand.

I heard this a long time ago, and it really rang true to me, so I just kind of pass it along. Look, as long as you're doing the right thing, and somebody kind of messes you over or wrongs you, if you will, when you're doing the right thing, then holding on to anger or being upset or a grudge against that person, it's not hurting them, it's hurting you. So, basically, you are focusing your energy and all of your attention and intention on that negative force field, if you will. So if you just imagine it as a negative force field around your body that's just rejecting and stopping things from coming into your life because you are so focused and keened in on that person, those people, that job, that employer, that bank, or the economy, or whatever it is. And there's no space. There's no vacuum for space to open up, to bring and attract wealth and others things into your life because you're so focused on that negative energy.

Now, if you were screwing people over and messing people over, and then somebody messed you over, now, you got a grudge towards them, then you kind of "lit the fuse first." So, you probably deserve what we all probably deserve to have been screwed over if we were messing people over. But if you didn't do anything, and you are living a good life, and you are truly trying to just be a good person and doing the right thing...

I heard this a long time ago, "It's so simple in life. Just do what's right." We know the difference between right and wrong. We do what's right; we avoid what's wrong. And I always say, "Look, I'm not a really bright person with a high I.Q., but I know the difference between right and wrong. And I know that if I do things in my heart that I know aren't right, I won't like myself." And if I don't like myself, how can I expect others to like me and for good things to happen for me?

And you know, by the way, I always see people whether they're doing the right thing, and if they ever doubt, all I have to do is what I call "The Mirror Test." The Mirror Test is this: You and I have to look in the mirror every morning when we wake up and every night before we go to sleep. And the mirror does not lie about what it sees. You might be able to "pull the wool over other people's eyes," but you can't lie to the person looking at you in the mirror. And, eventually, it catches up to you.

So, back to your question, if you're holding this anxiety toward folks or this anger or this hostility knowing that you really didn't do anything and somebody made a bad decision and wronged you, it's not hurting that person; it's hurting you. And that happened to me. I was personally attacked after being on ABC's TV Show *Secret Millionaire*. It was just awful and nasty stuff by somebody that I thought was a friend of mine. And everybody was like "Go get him." Jonathan Sprinkles, one of our mutual, dear friends, he said this publicly in front of 600 people one time.

He said, "I've known James a long time. One of the proudest moments I ever have had being his friend and I was proud to be his friend, was when he was being personally attacked with really bad stuff about his family and everything. You know what James did to retaliate? Nothing."

And he said that was one of the most proud moments to be James's friend. And here's my point to this: There were people telling me I have to do this and I have to do that. And you know, granted that I had to get lawyers involved and that sort of thing for legal reasons. But putting out a smear campaign and attacking someone, and I just said, "Why? It's negative energy." Nothing is based on facts. It's all someone's hyped-up what he wants to say, and I am not going to stoop to that level, and I'm going to pray for him because obviously there's something that's within him that is causing him to be so angry at me. And then I found out later from others that I can't control that, and I'm not going to go through life worrying about that. The best I can do is pray for him and hope these things work out for him.

And, so, basically, it stopped bothering me at that point because I stopped resenting. Did I feel like I wanted to resent this person? Yeah, it's easy. We all fall into that.

▲Deborah: Sure.

▲James: In the end, I realized that would just consume my l life. And I got better, bigger things to do than worry about that stuff. So, I don't know if that helps anyone, but I really hope it does.

▲Deborah: Absolutely. Of course, of course. And what did you say, what was that thing about the storm? That would be a storm, right?

▲James: Yeah. That was a hurricane.

▲Deborah: I would say that definitely. And I have been in the hurricane, and I can imagine that would have been a hurricane for sure.

▲James: Yeah. It's the "What's the message in the storm?"

▲Deborah: Right!

Okay. What's the message in the storm? That's the way you're putting it, and I love that. For me, like you, and every other person on the planet, we've all had our challenge. We've all had maybe what we judge as very serious challenges like I would consider what you experienced with your sister. That would be at the top there. That would really at the top for me—something really huge, very challenging, and a big opportunity for sure. And then there's stuff that's maybe not as challenging, but we've all had some sort of challenge. I don't think anyone is immune. And one of the things I loved to do is "Find the Gold" in the storm.

So, how did you learn to do that because it is a mindset piece to take an— unsavory? That's the word I'm getting right now – unsavory situation. That's a really sweet way that we're being told to say it. An *unsavory* situation—and find something sweet within it, right?

So, I can imagine, like with your sister, and I'm sure you found a lot of gold from that, even though it was probably one of the most painful things you've gone through in your life. So, how do you talk about that with others, and how do you teach that to others, and then is there a special process or something you do within yourself to get to that point? Yeah, in the beginning, sure, we might want to react, we're sad, we're angry, or we're frustrated, but eventually to move through that storm we got to do something.

▲James: All I can do, and I thought long and hard about this like, "How do I help other people with this?" And honestly, Deborah, I had no clue.

▲Deborah: Ha! Can't this be one of your 50 ways? There are 50 ways, and I'm not sure which one works.

▲James: What I mean by that is that all I actually can do is tell folks what works for me and maybe that inspires them, and it works for them in some way. But I really have thought, how do I help people through this? And I have resolved to the fact after a few years of trying to figure it out that I can't, I don't know, and I have no clue. So the only thing I can hope to do is tell what works for me, and maybe it gives them an idea or that thing that works for me works for them. But as far as coaching someone on how to get through that and "find the gold" in the storm, honestly, I have not found a clue on how I can do that. Now, other people can, but I can't. So let me tell you what works for me, and maybe it will work for someone else.

▲Deborah: Absolutely. We'll combine yours and mine and give it to the people in the book.

▲James: Yeah, exactly. Again, it comes back to what I said earlier, I always think about my sister – number one. That was probably the hardest thing I have ever seen in my life. I think, deep down, even though she was trying to believe and think positively, I think she knew. You kind of know your body, you know yourself, you know your spirit, and I think she sort of knew that that was the end for her. But never once did she moan or complain or say "Why me?" and I'm thinking, "My gosh, that is like the most difficult, toughest thing I've ever seen somebody go through over a three- or a four-month period." And if she felt that way and always was upbeat and happy, what am I complaining about? So, that's the first thing.

Number two: Somebody somewhere is always going through a more difficult time than I'm going through, no matter how tough my situation is.

Number three: I always say to myself, "What positive-ness can possibly come out of me being negative and dwelling on it and holding grudges and all that stuff?" That's just negative energy that bottles up. It's like a volcano, right? It bottles up, bottles up, bottles up for months and sometimes in years and years and years, and next thing you know it explodes, right? And I look at it the same way. I'm like, "What good is going to come from being negative? What good is going to come from having negative vibes and energy towards someone or things, or people, or the economy, or what's going on in the news?" Nothing positive is going to happen from that, so I choose to not be that way.

And those are three things that just work for me.

▲**Deborah:** Love it. It's very clear, concise, and do-able. Definitely something to think about. It's an invitation. And as you tell your story, I mean it invites this possibility. That's what I'm definitely getting from this. You're inviting that there is something positive that someone can extract even if it's as simple as my life may not be as hard as someone else's is right now and just to open up to that it's beautiful, James. I love that.

And that's a huge piece about shifting your mindset. I mean so much of it is about what we're thinking, what we're judging, what we believe, and all of that. I know you have a really fun story about a previous girlfriend and a Valentine's gift, right? And it was some sort of colon cleanse. And what I do know about you is you're very positive about health, and that was a very loving thing to do, right?

So, I know you're all about cleansing the body, detoxify it. And then to you, that would be a Spiritual AND Wealthy plus, right? I love that story.

And, so, what are your thoughts about the idea of detoxifying our brain: keeping away the toxins that are produced from negative thinking, from our limited beliefs, our fear and worry? How much are those things impacting someone's spirituality and their wealth?

▲**James:** Okay. Well, first of all, let me clarify the "Giving the girlfriend a bottle of colon cleanse."

▲**Deborah:** It's just such a good story, James.

I AM

▲**James:** First of all, let me preface it by saying that was quite a long time ago when I was in college.

▲**Deborah:** Yes, you were young.

▲**James:** And let me say, I like to think I learned since then. Okay?

▲**Deborah:** There was no mistake. There was something positive that came from that, yes.

▲**James:** And, just to be perfectly clear for anyone who might be reading or listening, that I did it out of love and caring.

▲**Deborah:** Totally! No, totally, I get it. I was not even trying to joke around about it. I totally believe that is completely true, absolutely.

▲**James:** So, basically what it was, in a nut shell is, then I will answer your question, was, I was so much in the health and working out because I was a collegiate athlete then, and I started cleansing a lot because someone told me — I believe it was a holistic-type practitioner said — if you cleanse and get the toxins out of your colon and other internal organs, your body will function better, and you'll be quicker, as an athlete. You'll have more stamina and so on. And I always look for the edge – anything that I could do that was legal to get the edge in basketball. And I said, "Alright, I'll try."

And I went on this herbal cleanse, and I just felt so much better when the toxins got released from my body. And, so, I thought, because I cared for this girl in college, that maybe I would get her to start cleansing with me. But dummy me; I didn't realize that you're not supposed to give a girlfriend a bottle of Colon Cleanse for her *Valentine's Day* gift.

▲**Deborah:** Maybe not.

▲**James:** It took a long time to come out that doghouse, I tell you. But it's a very simple process. So, if you think about cleansing your mind, your heart, your soul, your spirit, it's no different than cleansing the toxins out of your body. And it's very simple how someone explained this to me years ago. So, I will relate it to help with cleansing your colon, which is not a nasty thing; it's a very healthy thing. But they said, "Do you have a sink in your apartment?" And I said, "Well, of course, I do." They said, "Has your sink ever gotten backed up like it clogged up and you couldn't put water down?" And I said, "Well, sure!"

So that is how our body gets. And what clogs up your sink that could cause your pipes to erode and really harm your entire sink and all the pipes and all the mechanisms under it are the same sort of thing. Toxins, if you will, can cause your organs to be harmed, which means you are not going to run properly, your body won't function properly, and it could even shorten your lifespan. But just as you would use some sort of Liquid Plumber's stuff to clean out the pipes, so everything flows right, you got to clean the toxins out of all areas of your body, so your body runs right. And to me that made a lot of sense.

And, so, how does that relate to your mind or to people who are around in an environment? Well, we get polluted with different types of toxins. Some of them are in the forms of people we think are our friends that we've allowed to pollute our lives.

I always use this analogy when I do my talks for corporations and associations. I always ask, "How many of you have fish, like in a tank?" And some people would put their hands up and I'll say, "When fish are sick in the tank, how do you treat the fish to get them better? And don't say, 'Flush them down the toilet.'" And they'll say, "Take them to the fish doctor." And I'm like, "Where the heck is the fish doctor?" They'll say, "Give some pills to the fish." And I say, "No, you don't understand."

You don't actually treat the fish. You cleanse the environment; you cleanse the pollutants out from the tank around them. Well, how is it any different for you and I? There might be people who are polluting your mind or polluting your spirit. You may be polluting your own mind, your own heart, and your own spirit by the thoughts you think, by the actions you take or don't take. And you've got to have a snap-out-of-it phase where you just wake up and say, "I got to stop polluting myself for letting others pollute me. And I got to do a cleanse here because, if not, those toxins in the form of negativity, in the form of people putting you down, in the form of not aligning with the higher source whatever is right for you, not being around positive people who are lifting you up and trying to help you. Those toxins are going to start to weigh you down and pull you down. So, you always have to mentally cleanse, if you will.

▲**Deborah:** Absolutely. We need a mental cleanse bottle like your Colon Cleanse. Wouldn't that be easy? That's the magic bullet everyone is looking for.

It takes effort to do that. It takes some doing. Again, it is: sit in your lotus position but also be mindful of what you're thinking and what you're allowing into your environment.

▲**James:** Absolutely.

▲**Deborah:** Love it!

▲**James:** Yeah. It sounds strange, but it all comes back to this—taking personal responsibility. Yes, people may wrong you. People may pollute you, but you have a choice to let it keep going on or you have a choice to forgive and forget and move on. You have a choice to not hang around certain individuals who are polluting you.

It's like this. You walk into, like I live in Las Vegas, and you go into an area of a casino where people are smoking. Well, I don't like the fact they're smoking. I personally despise smoking. Now, that's just my opinion. But you know what? It's permitted in that casino, so I can't stop it, but if I choose to go sit down next to people who are smoking, whose fault is it? It isn't theirs; it's mine.

And it's the same way for allowing things to continue on in our lives that are polluting us. You may not be able to stop certain things, but when it comes to a point where you make a choice just like I can make a choice to go sit in that casino and be around that smoke, even though I hate it and that I can moan and complain, I'm choosing to pollute myself because I could choose to not be there.

▲**Deborah:** Oh, absolutely. I love it.

And, James, I know you told stories about—true stories, of course—where you lived in a really small apartment, financially not doing as well as you currently are today. What do you think for you personally that you could share that might help some else, what do you think was—maybe not *the*—but one area of your own thinking, that you needed to let go or detoxify? What was one of your anchors that had to go so that you could really open up to really receiving the abundance of God that's here for all of us?

▲**James:** Well, I had to, it might sound a little strange, but I had to think of myself in a different way.

▲**Deborah:** That doesn't sound strange to me at all.

▲**James:** And what I mean by that is, it all came down to one thing, and this was a real kick in the shins for me, so to speak, is when I had to realize that everything I had or didn't have in some way I created it. I was making $18,000 a year living in Southern California in a bad apartment with bars on the window, sleeping with a softball bat at night in case somebody broke in, and eating Top Ramen Noodles.

Well, maybe at that point, that's kind of where I started, but I created that. I chose to live in that area. I chose the financial path that I was on because I chose the career. I chose to go hangout on Friday and Saturday nights with friends, going out and partying instead of going and sitting my butt in a bookstore and reading all night Friday and all day and night Saturday, which I eventually then did. But in the beginning, I didn't do any of that stuff. I didn't try to better myself. I didn't try to change my thinking.

You see, your thoughts impact everything you do, good or bad. I mean it really starts right there. It's like the fuse that gets lit that everything else comes from. And it wasn't until I realized I had to change me and that I was responsible for where I was, where I wasn't, what I have, what I didn't have, and where I was going. And there was nobody else. Nobody did it to me. Nobody was dictating the direction of my future.

When I realized that everything came down to me and how I was attracting it, good or bad in my life, I realized I need to change and be the person that I want to actually be. And I need to have it before I will have it because it will attract to me. A lot of folks say "Law of Attraction," and when I teach I try to make a very simple analogy and say, "You have to have it before you'll have it. You have to have it your mind before you'll have it in a physical realm."

So, just to give you an example, I used to take pictures of great motivational speaker Zig Ziglar. Mr. Ziglar would be in front of 10,000 people in a picture or maybe 20,000. And I took a picture of myself, and I cut it out and I pasted in my face my head on his body. And I pasted it up. This is when I was broke, living on that dingy apartment. And I pasted it on the bathroom mirror because I said, "Man, I got to look in this bathroom mirror every morning when I wake up and every night before I go to sleep. I don't want to see who I am; I want to see who I'm going to be. And I'm going to be speaking like Mr. Ziglar someday. I don't know how I'm going to do it." But you see, I started changing how I saw myself. And it was tough. It was tough. I'm not saying it was easy. But what's the alternative? To sit in that apartment eating Top Ramen Noodles, saying, "Woe is me"?

▲**Deborah:** Not so sexy.

▲**James:** For me, the answer to your question, Deborah, is when I had to change how I thought about myself.

▲**Deborah:** I love it, which is huge because we all often begin to listen to other people's negativity, their comments, maybe their projection throughout our life and then we take all that baggage on, by choice. Sometimes we don't realize we're choosing that, but once you realize that you have a choice about how you are going to think about yourself and others and, talk about freedom, I think that's a huge freedom piece for those of us who are out there teaching. We realize, like for me, I used the words when I realized I was at my own jail keeper. I was the one keeping myself in jail. It's like the clouds parted. I just went, "Oh my God, this is what I've been doing."

And from that moment forward, when you have some awareness about that, life definitely changes for sure. But I am glad you're not eating Top Ramen Noodles anymore. Although, I must say my son when he was younger, he thought, "When I go to college, I'm going to save a lot of money. I'm going eat nothing but Top Ramen Noodles." And I assure you, he's in college, and he is not eating Top Ramen Noodles. His own mindset has definitely shifted.

Well, one of the things you talked about right there James was this idea of creating these precise images of the person you are stepping into where you wanted to, what you wanted to become. And I wonder of a lot of the things that you consider some of your greatest success and maybe achievements maybe even the home you purchased, anything in your life that you have really, really wanted. How precise did you get about your scene that you're imagining it, you're visualizing it?

▲**James:** It's like the first key of when I start anything. It's like the first thing, first step, I do. It's going to sound kind of funny, but I say, "How am I going to make this work out?"

I remember telling this to somebody one time; I was in this business thing. And I said to myself, "How am I going to make this work?" And then he was like, "Well, what do you mean? It, just works out." And I said, "No, it works out that way I want it to work out." At first I start to see it. You have to see it before you'll ever have it, right? It comes back to my little line "You got to have it before you'll have it." And I believe a principle called "Act as if." You act as if you already have it. So, because if you study the subconscious mind, your subconscious mind does not know the difference between fiction and reality. So you might as well picture how you want things even though that's not reality because your subconscious doesn't know the difference and your subconscious is the GPS, if you will, that helps tune in to the frequency that will help you to attract what you want.

So, everything from the house I have now, I actually am looking at it up on my vision board where I have a picture of the view of my exact balcony that I have now. And that picture was put up, I bet you, three years before I ever decided to buy this land and build a house. And it was just crazy — or it's not crazy, as you and I understand it but —

▲**Deborah:** Yeah, I know. It's just wild and amazing.

▲**James:** Yeah, exactly. So, the first step for me is to picture how I'm going to make it end up. That sounds weird because things just happened. Nope, nope! They happen to the way you orchestrate them, I believe.

▲**Deborah:** Absolutely. You're co-creating it, for sure. It's like, "Hey here's my list, this is what I want," and believing that it's possible.

And, so, you have that type of picturing and maybe words or whatever. You have that some place where you are seeing it on a daily basis. Is that correct?

▲**James:** Oh, yes, absolutely. I have them, and I'm looking at it right now in my office.

Let me tell you this, Deborah, because I don't if a lot of people do it this way, but I do it a little differently. So, my office is where I have my business and my financial pictures and not only pictures but words that tie into the pictures. But my bedroom is where I have my family, my relationship, and my spiritual words and pictures.

▲**Deborah:** Brilliant!

▲**James:** I don't take my business into my like personal space, if you will, and vice versa. I keep my personal stuff separate from my business stuff.

And I actually remember telling Jack Canfield that, the co-creator of *Chicken Soup for the Soul*, and he's on the movie, *The Secret*, you know, the one with the Law of Attraction. I remembered Jack saying, "Actually I don't know if I've ever heard of anybody doing that before."

▲**Deborah:** Most people put it all together. Right! It's brilliant.

▲**James:** And I have my bag that I take with me to the gym, when I go the gym to work out. And inside my bag, I have my health and my fitness goals, my pictures, and my words in my bag, so when I'm at the gym and in that space, that's where I'm seeing those.

▲**Deborah:** I love it. So, you're quite precise about what you desire.

▲**James:** Correct. Yeah. I mean it's like, how do you hit something, if you're just scattered all over the place? The metaphor is you need to look through a scope and be very specific about what you're looking at to see.

▲**Deborah:** Right, absolutely. And it's so amazing how many people, and my clients, and I'm sure you have this too, where I go, "Okay so what is it that you want?" And they're hardly moving. They don't even have an idea. Deep down, they have some ideas, but they kind of put them away. They've tucked them away as maybe impossible. And like that extracting of helping them to draw out what their true desires are because often they don't have that precise vision yet. And so, no wonder their life is a little scattered as you were saying, for sure.

▲**James:** Well there's a quote a long time ago that I've always liked. I forgot who said it. I think it was anonymous when I heard it, but it said, "If you don't know where you're going, how can you expect to get there?"

▲**Deborah:** Exactly. Amen!

▲**James:** It's simple. It's kind of like, "Fly to a place you've never been. Get a rental car and then just drive—plus, you got an hour drive. Just try to drive to the destination you've never been to before without having a map or a GPS, and see how quickly you get there."

▲**Deborah:** Exactly. Love it. Well, I would love to wrap up with just kind of a popcorn thought or whatever comes up.

You know that when I first saw you, my very first meeting with you, one of the things you supported me on was just really extracting out "What am I passionate about?" And what came out of that meeting was really part of the birth of this book and my work in a deeper, deeper level.

And I said, "Well, you know, James, I just want people to know and to be able to live this idea of 'It's OK to be Spiritual AND Wealthy.'" And it was like we just stopped. The room stopped at that moment. And you're like, "Well, then just do that, Deborah." Right?

So when you hear that, it's like so simple, right? When you hear that tag line, the title of this book *It's OK to be Spiritual AND Wealthy,* what are your first thoughts? What would like to share about that?

▲**James:** Well, the first thing is, personally for me, I'm so proud of you for actually grasping that and doing it because I think it's so needed, number one. And you're the perfect soul to give people permission that it's okay to be both because I think, forever, people have seesawed back and forth on, "Well, I can only one be one or the other." And when we sat here, and you sort of said that, and I said, "Well, I would read that because I wrestled with that, and we all wrestle with that."

So the first thought is, I'm so excited, and I just can't wait to see how many people you are going to impact with this whole message and movement. It's not a message; it's a movement. So that's the first thing.

The second thing is, you're just going to help so many folks who have been wrestling with this for years, and you are going to instantly stop that with them to where they say, "Oh my gosh. Okay, I'm spiritual, I can be wealthy, and I won't be bad person if I'm both." Think about that. That's going to be very, very cool.

▲**Deborah:** I love it. Thank you.

▲**James:** So, that's what really comes to mind first. I couldn't think of a better messenger than you to deliver this because I think it's so right-on with who you are and what you're trying to do to help people. From a business standpoint, also, it's great. It's so catchy, if you will, because so many people wrestled with that and have for years.

Number three: It's when you explain it and teach and coach in the way that you do so well, it's almost as if people instantly stop battling within their spirit, and the lid is released, and they are free. So those are the three things that I see.

▲**Deborah:** Ya, and freedom is really what it is all about.

I love it. James, thank you so very much. I have absolutely enjoyed this conversation and listening to your wisdom and sharing even on deeper levels—your share about your sister. And, often, we think we're doing things for certain reasons and, yes, I absolutely want to get this book out and share more with the world and all of that. But what I also realized along the way is there's these wonderful little pockets of the unexpected mystery that come up and your heartfelt share about your sister, that part of the story I've never heard, just that was worth all of this, truly.

▲**James:** Well, thank you, Deborah and thank you for having me. I can't wait to read the book.

▲**Deborah:** Heck, yeah! Thank you so much.

▲**James:** Thank you!

David Wood
Strategic Consultant
www.amplifiedliving.com

David Wood has developed world-class personal development training programs that have impacted hundreds of thousands of people. He is a Business Leader, Author, Trainer and Humanitarian who has lived, traveled and worked in over 50 countries. He brings his passion for people, culture and the unknown into everything that he does.

David was a lead trainer for Peak Potentials Training, the fastest and largest growing personal development company in the world and is internationally recognized as the "Trainer's Trainer." He has grown several multi-million and million-dollar companies and currently is a strategic consultant for Isagenix, a 1.5 Billion-Dollar health and wellness company out of Phoenix, Arizona.

As a Trainer and Speaker, he brings his global experience and deep understanding of the human condition to create some of the most dynamic, engaging, fun and effective training events. He is known for his uncanny ability to read his audience and move people to the next level in their lives.

David works with thousands of trainers, teachers and educators, and has a goal to personally train 10,000 trainers who are committed to delivering transformational work.

As a Humanitarian, David is a spokesperson, fundraiser and advocate for the Make-a-Wish Foundation and has raised millions of dollars for children in need.

David would tell you, however, that his greatest accomplishment is being the father of his two boys, Calvin and Ben.

Deborah "Atianne" Wilson's Interview with David Wood

▲**David:** Hi, Deborah.

▲**Deborah:** Good Morning. Hey! Good morning, David!

▲**David:** How are you?

▲**Deborah:** I'm good. What a pleasure and honor I get to play and co-create with you again. Thank you so very much.

▲**David:** No problem. How is the sound? I put it through my recording studio. I put it through there, as opposed to on the phone, so I thought maybe a richer sound play.

▲**Deborah:** Yes, no worries, no worries because we're going to transcribe it anyway. So lovely. Thank you so much for thinking about it—so appreciate it, and truly I have so much fun with you. I just felt what a lovely excuse I get to interview you from my book, and I get to connect and co-create again. I love it.

And I've listened to your podcast, by the way: the one you did right after we did our interview; the one where you shared about the fire walk, and then the bird, and the wonderful story that you alluded to when we were connecting, and I have tell you, David, what I love about you, what I just connected in so deeply during our conversation and listening to your podcast, is you are exuding such a huge energy of being genuine that I just find extraordinary. And I had to share that with you, and I mean it's a beautiful—it's a beautiful word and world to be revealed to me about you. It's just—and I don't how that resonates with you, but I had to start our conversation out with just saying how beautiful that energy is around you and in you.

▲**David:** Thank you. Well, I mean that's one of the big things I'm passionate about teaching is the authenticity, so I hope that comes across.

▲**Deborah:** Yes, absolutely, and it did. It's just—it's so interesting because often the word authenticity is definitely what comes up, but for you, I'm seeing it even deeper. It's like this—and, again, and I don't know a lot about you, but I've peeked in now, and I've heard stories from you, but *genuine* seems even deeper. It just seems like it's really landed so deeply within you and such a great place to teach others, so I'm just going to say thank you to you for all you do in the world with your programming and the work you do on stage and everything.

▲**David:** Thank you so much.

▲**Deborah:** Thank *you*.

▲**David:** Here's my deal, just so you know, I do have another call I got to go on, and so I'm going to give you as much time as you need so, but, well, I mean—as soon as I can. They know I'm going to be late, so I mean I may end up going to rush you, or we can do in two parts, so we just need to be efficient, that's all.

▲**Deborah:** You got it. I'm all about efficiency, so let's go. I know your time is precious and you're traveling a lot, so let's jump in. So, I jotted down a couple of areas that I intuitively thought we should play in, and what's interesting, because I put them in an order, but Spirit has its own wonderful progression, and the first place I'd love for you to share some of your wonderful wisdom is in the area of forgiveness.

Forgiveness of self, forgiveness of others and how much this might come up in the work that you do, whatever's happened with you and your own world? Really, this place of how has forgiveness impacted your life from getting from where you were perhaps. You know, from when you were maybe traveling the world, and to where you are now.

David: Sure, sure. Well I think it's a great question. What happened to me personally is I grew up in a very sort of a dark energy; there was a lot of abuse, there was a lot of, I say, real hatred of my mom. My dad and my mom separated when I was seven. And my dad left my mom for her best friend, so what happened was there was a lot of hatred from my mom toward my dad and my dad's wife, who he's still married to today, which is like 46 years later, and also to his whole family, so there was a lot of this sort of darkness in the house.

So my mom also was, because she was sort of abandoned by him, she carried a lot of weight in her body and didn't know how to cope with each kid, and we were sort of left in the country, and so we ended up.... And then the only reason I'm giving you this context is because I think that forgiveness, when we talk about it generally, like if I say, "I've got to forgive you because you crashed into my car, or I've got to forgive you because you lied to me."

There were different levels of forgiveness, but I think the muscle is the same, and I think the one that we put in perspective. It doesn't matter how dark it was or how light it is; forgiveness is forgiveness. And that it has the same energy release or the same possibility to bring light to a situation.

So, just sort of to continue with that sort of journey.

My mom was abandoned in a foreign country. We ended up living in a condemned building, and it was just horrendous, especially for her, and there were rats, and the one room was completely boarded up because there was human excrement all over the wall. So, by Western standards, it was a really, really, a very, let's say, it was poverty by Western standards, which is hard to find because most people have TVs, and they have fridges, and they say they are in poverty. I mean I think poverty is relative.

So when my mom became quite violent, and she was always unpredictable, so as I grew up, I grew to hate her more and more and more. The last time we had a confrontation was she came to me with a vacuum cleaner pipe; she was going to hit me with. But then I picked up a stick, and I said, "If you do that again I'll knock your f***ing head." And that's kind of our relationship, right?

And then I left home at 15; at 18, I remember phoning her one time I'd been drinking, and I just said you're and I used a C-word and I hung up. That's kind of the extent. So just to give the context of what was going on inside me. And I started travelling around the world and for 10 ½ years; I had an amazing time, but this stuff was buried deep inside of me, and I had no real idea of the consequence of what I was carrying.

And on the surface, I had this incredible life. I'm traveling. I'm meeting new people. I'm making experiences. I'm opening up in so many ways. I went up to Canada; I was sort of illegal here, but I ended up falling in love with this girl, and she was the one that introduced this concept of forgiveness to me, and she sat with me one day.

She said, "You realize...." And she could see the way I was treating her, I mean I was a great—I was a fun lover, I was all these things, but I was very, very guarded deep down in the places within my heart; there was zero trust. I didn't realize at that time, but I didn't trust women because I had this experience, and there was no concept of that—zero.

She fortunately had been through some stuff herself, and she said, "You know, David, if you carry on like this, you're going to be a really lonely old man." And she said, "You know, have you ever thought about going back to England and just telling people how you feel?" I thought, well, that sounds all right.

You know, I was starting on this journey of at least personal discovery on a different level. I discovered the world. I discovered so much about myself, but on that deep, deep, deep level of intimacy, I hadn't really gone there because traveling around the world allows itself to fleeting relationships, which meant I could fall in love with someone, and they could fall in love with me; they knew I was traveling. It was like it was awesome; you'd have this wonderful time, they weren't disappointed because you were going, they knew that up in front. So it was perfect for a guy like me that was locked in, right?

▲**Deborah:** Right.

▲**David:** I decided that the trip to England would be valuable if I really wanted to step over this or to step through this kind feeling that was deep down inside, and, so, but she said something to me that changed everything. She said "Dave," she said, "you know, one thing you've got to understand," she said, "you can't expect anything to change and you can't expect them to change, and you can't expect them to agree and you can't expect them to say sorry." So, if you go there with any kind of expectation, you're going be sorely disappointed," she said, "but your job is to just forgive."

"And let them know what's going on and in that moment just forgive everything that's happened." Anyway, so I did that and exactly what she predicted happened. No one, whether it was physical abuse, whether it was sexual abuse, which I'd gone through all these different things; not one of the people really saw the incidents the same. No one saw, but I just shared what went on and in my world, I forgave.

And what happened, which was really incredible, is when I got back from England. I was staying with a friend of mine in London, Ontario. And I got to his house, and I collapsed and all this mucus. I mean it was just incredible, I got so sick, and I'm a guy that really, really—I mean very few people know me as ever being sick. I don't use medications; I never have. Anyway, so I collapsed, and I'm like I've got malaria, but I'm…. From every hour it's just my body that's just crap coming out of me, and it's like I've been holding on to something, and somehow it actually released out of my body in a physical way, which sounds a little woo-y, but it's what happened, right?

▲**Deborah:** Sure.

▲**David:** Then I started to really—I started doing personal development work about 13 years ago I actually did some forgiveness work, where I actually did some forgiveness techniques, and I started working with different leaders in the area of forgiveness, and Larry Gilman who works with the sort of the releasing of your authentic self, and then I worked with Harv Eker and did some other forgiveness practices.

What I realized was there were still a lot of residuals, residual things lying around in my closet that I never really understood the importance of total forgiveness. So I coined the term, which I believe I live in every moment, which is "immediate forgiveness", and immediate, by the way, could be a few days. It could be a week. It could be whatever, but immediate means that I'm not willing—I mean if I'm in pain, if I'm having a fight with someone like a— by the way, I don't fight a whole lot, but let's say I'm having an argument with Jen, my partner, and that happens from time to time where we have a misunderstanding and, typically, within five or ten minutes, it's over, right?

But there are occasions where it may take a couple of days to sort itself out, but that's very, very rare. So, I can stay in it if I need to, if there's something I need to get off my chest, or we don't have the right.... maybe the opportunity doesn't present itself to have a conversation. In which case the energy of what's going on is still lingering because you we talked about it.

And then, what I'll do is I'll completely let go, and so what I gotten in my life is understanding that, you know, I use this saying a lot, you know, "holding on to something." Holding on to anger, disappointment, resentment, holding on to judgment—all these things is like drinking poison and expecting the other person to die.

And so now, I go to a place where it's immediate forgiveness. And what I feel is so right because two things will happen; one is that if there's something going on, I'll address it. If I've got something going on with someone, I'll find a chance to speak to them. And, typically, I take a 100% responsibility for my part of it. So, I don't use the word *blame* because you can't have the word *blame* and *forgiveness* in the same sentence. You know, well, it's your fault, but I forgive you. That's not what it is about.

So what I learned is, first of all, to forgive myself for all of my weaknesses and my idiosyncrasies—that's why there's no regret in my life because I've realized all the mess-ups I've made. And I've made a lot, and I continue to make mess-ups. You know, it's just part of my own growth thing, and my intention is not to deliberately hurt people. And when I do, I have the where with all to go and say, "Guess what, Dave? Your intention was not to deliberately hurt that person. So you've hurt him, go clean that up but don't hold on to it. Forgive yourself, learn the lesson, don't do it again or do your best not to. And if you do, I'll give you a serious talking to."

▲**Deborah:** Right. Oh, my gosh. Yeah, and that's what makes you so genuine in these moments. It's huge. And so, in the celebration really of your story which, thank you so much for sharing about your childhood, and that's really opening up that vulnerability page and just really being so transparent, and I honor that, and I just really, really appreciate it. I mean these are the kind of conversations that I just adore.

I want to ask you in regard to celebration. So you just mentioned this is really what we would consider quite an intense, quite a negative, obviously, experience as a child. And I wonder with that and even what you call your mess-ups, right, which we all continue to do these wonderful experiences we have that we can learn from and we can grow from, and we do expand.

Can you celebrate who you are today because of those experiences and especially with family life? A lot of people have a lot of deep regret and pain and sorrow—wounds around family life, their upbringing. And so, who are you that you can celebrate today, something that came from that childhood experience? How has that made you this amazing man you are today?

▲David: Let me be clear on the question, though. Can you—just so I can answer the way you want it. I'm not sure I have....

▲Deborah: Sure, sure, sure. Because I was rambling, of course, no, no, no. So we have these experiences like your childhood, and there's a lot of pain, and there's a lot of suffering in the moment and stuff and we get past; you've come to this place of forgiveness. And I'm wondering, can you celebrate what you've learned?

▲David: Here's what I'll tell you, and the validation of this is the amount of shows I do. I'll give you an example: I just did a show, I've done two shows this week with two different, a couple actually, one who has gone through severe depression, suicidal almost depression and sort of popped out the other side and is now an author and a tremendous advocate for the whole depression kind of conversation. And she's a world-class athlete, but she really has found a pathway through the darkness. And for 25 years, she was stuck there and in drugs, in alcohol, and all the other things that come along.

Her partner was crushed by a rock, a 2,000-pound rock in a remote part of Australia and spent 45 hours pinned under this rock in a waterbed where his life was really, really in peril. When they finally rescued him, they amputated both his legs.

So, this is a good example of a couple who have gone through monumentally different things. Each of them, with the possibility to determine a life course that could be of regret, of "poor me," of any kind of a victim kind of mentality, yet both of them have ... I asked them this question before they released, I said, "Let me ask you the question." This is the question: Would you go back and not want to go through depression, or would you go back and not want to lay under that rock for 45 hours and your life imperiled, getting eaten by ants and crayfish. I mean crayfish were coming out of the water and eating his foot. I mean, it was just a crazy, crazy story.

And both of them said the same thing: "I wouldn't change a thing." And, for me, I would not want anything to change. I would not because the empathy that I have and the understanding I have of people is born in the very fires of those things that may seem harsh.

I think Eckhart Tolle says this. He says that, "truly, the people that end up finding and living their purpose typically have gone through the most horrendous things in their life." And the horrendous actions or the horrendous journey that awakens in them the desire to create change and the desire to step into something greater to play a role in a much bigger game in life.

So, for me, there is not a second, there's not one conversation, there's not one beating, there's not one piece of abuse or anything that went on in my whole life or anything that I did. I mean I was a thief, I was a liar, I was in jail, I was doing drugs, I was on alcohol. I mean none of it. I wouldn't change one tiny thing because all of that is a culmination of my life experience that allows me to sit in so many situations with such a "Hey, I have no judgment."

I have zero judgment of anyone because I have zero judgment of myself. I'm not sitting and beating the crap out of myself and that's what I say. If someone is highly judgmental, I know that the quiet conversation in their head is one of judgment, and they spend more time beating the shit out of themselves than they do anything, that's why they beat the shit out of everyone else around them.

So yeah, the celebration is, and I think if people understood it especially people who are reading this book, if they understood the fact that it's the very thing you are going through that later on you're going to look back on, and it may be years, it maybe decades. You're going to look back on and you say, "Oh, thank God that happened. Wow, I would never change that."

When you're in it, you are like *just get me out of this hell-hole*. This is wrong, why me? You are in your pity party, right? But it's later on you realize the magic of those moments. And I don't think there's ever a moment, unless someone takes their own life and they get lost in it. You know, that could happen when you get so absorbed by it all that you end up either taking your own life; or, you don't find a way out, you stay stuck in the victim. And that's those people who will blame, justify, and complain. They stay in a victim conversation the rest of their life.

I AM

Those kind of people, they do get stuck, but with those of the people reading this right now, then it's really a question of making you the most important investment and focusing on a new journey and truly finding a reason or purpose – a bigger calling. And I think no one I've met, who's great—really great—hasn't gone through adversity.

▲**Deborah:** Absolutely amen to that, truly, truly. I love that because just like you, I've had my own intense experiences, sexual abuse, and cancer, and there's a list. And the beauty of that that I see now is to be able to sit with those very people who've had similar experiences, something in that realm and to be able to show them, "I've been there. I've had my own turning points, and I'm on the other side." And this light-filled path that you can show people, very humbly, that they can go there too. And that's just...

▲**David:** And the beauty is—I think the beauty is—that it's not that you have to say anything, but there's an understanding and a non-conscious conversation that goes on between people. And people who, because some people get stuck in their story, but I think that what happens is, when you're around people, they feel something because of the empathy, because of the lens that you're looking at their life through. There is something even if the conversation never comes up, there's a feeling of connection and they're not quite sure why. Right?

▲**Deborah:** Oh, absolutely. I find it amazing that so many people that have been attracted to my work have such similar stories. They are where I've been, and I'm sure you've seen that as well in your work, too.

So, David, in this celebration piece and this idea you were talking about, you know, when we're in it, like when we're in the thick of it like right now, Colorado, Boulder, we're in the thick of this "natural disaster." There's flooding, there's devastation, there's death—all these things that we would call horrific experiences for people and at the same time, we both know often in that moment, you can't see that light.

And, so, I'm wondering, what is it that happened for you along your journey that helped you go from more of that victim consciousness that shifted your mindset because I know you're definitely about mindset in whatever words you used around that and shifting your beliefs and understanding so that you can really live this kickass life that you live.

▲**David:** I think there are a few things, but I think it's finding your purpose and calling. In the end, I think like I said, "What's born in those times." Well, let me talk about the flood. I've been in floods and natural disasters. And what it brings out typically is the best in people.

We had big fires here, where 430 homes were burned down in their hometown here. One of my friends lost his house. And I remember saying to him I said, "Rick," I said, "You know what? You can't see it right now but one day you're going to say to me, 'Dave, I'm so glad that happened.'" But it's impossible because he lost everything. I mean his house was burned down.

I remembered seeing him three years later, and we were sitting having a cup tea and he says, "Dave, I can't believe how great that was." I said, "What do you mean?" He said, "It felt like I had this cleanse. All this shit that I was carrying around in my life was gone." He said, "The insurance came in and helped me build this new house. We got a pool, which we didn't have."

Again, not everyone has insurance, I get that. But I can tell you again on how many people who let go of the story, the victim story that they are in because some people you see them 10 years after their partner embezzled a hundred thousand dollars, and they're still freaking talking about it.

▲**Deborah:** Right, right. Yeah.

▲**David:** The reason why I'm here is because Jim embezzled my money. No! The reason you're here is because you never got over the freaking fact that Jim embezzled your money, and you stayed stuck in that silly story. So what if he embezzled your money?

So I think there's a choice that we have to make like whether it's losing a love one. I lost a 10-year-old in my family, which was devastating. So, again, having that experience when people lose kids; I mean, I understand what it feels like to have that situation going in your life. You don't know how completely to understand their situation but what happens is this.

We have to choose at some point whether the story is going to become a defining moment and something we will definitely look back on and say, "Wow, you know what? I found the best in myself, you know, when this flood happened in the town I lived."

I remember being up all night and carrying people out to a hospital, and sandbagging, and the community coming together, and everyone collapsing at 7:30 in the morning, dirty and close. And the whole community felt like it was beating with one heart.

And for months and months and months later, everyone kept looking back at that time and saying "Wasn't that great? Wasn't it great how everyone came together?" And it wasn't like, shit, we lost some houses and people, you know, yeah, some people die. I mean people die every single day, and we just got to get over the fact that people die. And sometimes it's horrific, but I think a lot of us get stuck in the idea that we're not going to die. And this is part of the problem that we can't move on.

I go on the mindset that I have no idea if I'm going to be alive at the end of the day. So, I have to live my life fully in this day. I can't expect my life to be starting next week on Tuesday when I've decided to feel better. I have to deal with my stuff today knowing that this could be my last day, knowing that this could be my last breath.

I think that gives me a lot of freedom in that I have never taken it for granted that I was going to live a long life. I live the life I'm in knowing that it could end and I'm ready. I always say and this is something that I've done for many, many years; I've already thought about what I'm going to be like if I get burned or if I become a paraplegic, a quadriplegic, if I lose all my functions, if I become incontinent, if I get Stage 5 cancer and die in six weeks; I know exactly how I'm going to act because I've made the decision. And how do I know that? Well, because I have enough examples out there.

You know "The Man in Motion," who is a guy who became a paraplegic. He was hitchhiking; he was a very, very famous Canadian. Rick Hansen is his name. And a toolbox hit in the back, became a paraplegic young guy. And what did he do? He becomes an ambassador and he wheels his wheelchair around and the world, and he brings awareness to people in wheelchairs. And he lives an incredible life. He is a bestselling author. He met the woman of his dreams.

You know Nick Vujicic was born with no arms and no legs—a guy that found his purpose, and he found his voice. He's had his first baby. He never thought he could marry someone. His wife is *gorgeous*, both from the inside and the outside. And he's a guy with no arms and no legs. And he says, "I've got this little chicken drumstick."

And I can give you a hundred examples. Christopher Reeve, you know, Superman then he breaks his third vertebrae or whatever; he becomes a quadriplegic on a ventilator. And some of his best work happened after that.

So, I know that there are people that wake up after a devastating accident and they focus on, "Alright, now what?" And same that happened with this guy that I talked about he lost both his legs in his interview. And he wouldn't go back, to wanting his legs back, because the very fact he lost his legs is he found a voice. And he's in the Guinness World Records for the first double amputee to summit Kilimanjaro. And now like 13 people a year do it. And he says, "I feel like I have this whole world now like it has opened up to me that never existed before.

▲**Deborah:** Absolutely, absolutely. And you're right, and I love that you have traveled the world, and you have so many of these stories because it goes back to the idea of what you said the mindset of "It is a choice," for sure. And I have the sassy saying.

In fact, I was talking with Beth, our mutual friend, and I just said I want this big screen that says "So What! Now What?" And it's not without compassion, it's not without empathy. But the fact is where you are is where you are. So now what do you want to do with it. And that's a mindset shift, and that's exactly what you're saying here.

▲**David:** Yeah, exactly.

▲**Deborah:** Okay, I know you have a lot to do. I'm going to ask you one more question. And it's in regard to the idea of "meditation," although I know that's a big trigger word for many people when I was on your show. Yeah, I referenced it as stillness in motion. And I just would love to hear your ideas about, your wisdom about, and even what your practice is and how important you feel it is to have these moments of stillness where you are connecting in or not. So, anything about that I would love to hear.

▲**David:** Well, my understanding of meditation has changed. I mean, I started meditating when I was 18. I fell in love with this girl called Linda, who was just kind of, she owned a natural health food store, and she was about 20 years older than me. She introduced me to a form of meditation through a guy called Maharaji, an Indian guru. And I went away for two or three days and learned how to meditate. And we have this thing called a beragon. And we'd sort of sit, and we would focus on our breath, and we'd focus on the light, and we'd focus on sounds with the ears, and we'd focus on the beat of the heart, right. So, there was these kind of four points to focus. Oh no, taste was the other one, not heart. It was taste, and we used to put our tongue back, in the back of our throat, so then it will be like a nectar, they called it. And this is like, oh, I'm 52, so that's 33 years ago or something.

And so what happened was, I've always had this kind of understanding because why I started traveling was I started meditating. And, remember, at that time I was drinking a lot, was getting high all the time, and all my friends were.... you know, every time you saw me I'd be rolling up a joint.

I met this girl; we go into this meditation thing. And we started practicing the meditation which is really, really unusual. We would sit sometimes for three or four hours with beautiful music on and just stare into each other's eyes. And it was like unbelievable, I almost felt like I could travel through her body. And I was experiencing this thing as a young man, and that there's a lot of intimacy between us, but it was like this a very, very powerful force. And we would do it for, I would say hours on end. And we did that a lot.

And, so, this started this whole journey. But what happened after I started meditating, I started writing. And I started writing this poetry. And the poetry, I mean one of my poems I wrote back then, I can probably still remember it, but I mean it's not real poetry. I mean, this is an 18-year-old writing or a 19-year-old writing stuff after meditating before getting high, right? The stuff I wrote is something like this:

> To be alone in a crowded room is there something wrong with me?
>
> How come the people around me don't see the things I see?
>
> It's easy to take another drink and obscure the life we've made
>
> And hide behind faded minds what stupid games we play
>
> Striving to accomplish to make our coffer full
>
> To build our little kingdom that we try in vain to rule
>
> And when we have our precious objects, it's then the trouble starts
>
> Because you can't take possessions with you
>
> When in this world you do depart
>
> And when the end of time had come, your life just slips you by
>
> Your mind was too preoccupied to ask quite simply why
>
> Why is my body breathing, what am I doing here
>
> Why not ask these simple questions, or is it the answers that you fear
>
> Fear because the material world and the power that we hold will simply have no meaning as our true life's quest unfolds

So I'm writing stuff like that, right? And...

▲**Deborah:** Wow! It's gorgeous.

▲**David:** Well, but I'm like this kid, and I'm starting to read my own writing. And it's what spurred me to leave the country. And, so, in this meditation, in this timeframe of me opening up my heart to something I've never experienced before... and remember, there's a lot of darkness around my world. I hate my Mom and like, you know, and I'm wigging out a lot, right? And so, in this sort of depth of my soul, I found the calling to go get the hell out of there. And that's why I started traveling, and I backpacked for 10 ½ years.

And so what I do is I typically, the way I meditate, it's become almost non-conscious. I wake up as soon as I—I've never used curtains—so, as soon the light creeps in the window of the house, so, typically this morning, it's about five, and I kind of wake up into a half state. And I lay, and when the house is completely quiet and there's no movement, there's no flow of energy anywhere except in my body. And I lay there, and I just have this deep connection to myself.

And what will happen is, quite often, a number of things will happen. Ideas pop into my head even though I'm not trying to think of them. These things come to me. And quite often, I even forget to write them down, but I just have this kind of deep well of understanding that comes to me.

Other times, I would just feel incredibly light and peaceful like I'm floating off the bed. And other times, I will actually fall into a deep, deep, deep sleep. But it feels like I'm in control of the sleep. I almost feel like I'm awake and asleep at the same time. I mean it's kind of almost passed out, but it feels like I'm having a conversation with the other person outside who is observing me. It's just odd, but I can steer the dreams, so it feels like I'm in control, okay? So I want this to happen. So now we're going paragliding. It doesn't matter, right?

And so I've done that.... that's the time that I find, because I lead a busy life that I connect with myself, and it's not a formal meditation. I don't sit with my legs crossed and chant.

The other type of meditation I do is I've always put myself into a very, very beautiful situations. And, so, what I do in the moment of a beautiful situation... so, gratitude is a form of meditation, so to sit in gratitude where it's not quieting the mind, but it's illuminating the mind through gratitude. Or, it's sitting on a vista and putting myself constantly in vistas that are breathtaking. And if I was to send you a photograph of the vista I'm looking at right now from my office, it is breathtaking.

And so, that in my other world is a form of meditation which is appreciation. So, gratitude and appreciation become a form of meditation in my life that serve me to have that same deep sense that I think meditation is all about. But

I'm not a real sitting-down-quietly in deliberate meditation, but I do a steady practice. It's just very loose.

▲**Deborah:** It's beautiful, and it goes back to what I call that *stillness in motion* because it can be so much more and that is part of definitely my teaching. It's to allow people to explore a variety of things that just can work for them like what you're saying. And beauty—I totally get what you're saying because I was, just even in the last months since I've spoken to you last, I was really feeling into, why is it I do what I do, and what is it that I want beyond this moment, you know, to have in life's experiences, should I be able to be blessed each and every day to wake up for many weeks, many more months, many more years.

And ultimately my biggest "Why" is about beauty—beauty in cultures, beauty in people, beauty in... And we're not talking superficial, we're not talking magazine beauty, right? We're talking about what you even shared on your show, basically the interview where you're teaching Beth to sail in that moment of pure bliss and gratitude in your life that it's just so extraordinary— so simple, moment of meditation, right? So beautiful.

▲**David:** Yeah, absolutely. I'm sending you a photograph right now.

▲**Deborah:** Alright. Oh great, I'm going to get to see what you're seeing. I love it.

▲**David:** Okay, wait a second. You know what I'm going to do is I'll just e-mail it to you. You're by the computer.

▲**Deborah:** I can be. Well actually yeah, absolutely.

▲**David:** Okay. Well, because I won't have time to actually punch it all in to get to you.

So there you go. This is what I'm looking at right now. I just want to give you the idea about what that means to me and why I choose to find these places in the world to rest my heart. I know it sounds a bit woo-y, but I'm a bit woo-y...

▲**Deborah:** No, are you kidding? You're talking to the queen of woo. There's something about woo. You know, when someone, when a man woos a woman, he is courting her, he is loving her, so to me woo is all about love. So that's just my take on it, for sure.

▲**David:** Yes, that's great language.

▲**Deborah:** You're so sweet. Okay, I'm opening up. I'm opening up, I'm waiting for it to come in.

So, while I'm waiting here for your beautiful vista, one of the things I just love about... to me what just happened is, you have no idea what my chapters are. I'm sure energetically you do, but what I love about the conversation that you shared so beautifully is that you covered so many of the keys I talk about without even me asking you, and I just love that—love when that happens. So thank you.

▲**David:** No worries.

▲**Deborah:** Oh my gosh! Okay, I'm seeing it David. It's extraordinary. Oh yeah, how beautiful. Beautiful. Absolutely...

▲**David:** Anyway, that's the view from my bedroom window. That's what I wake up to. So, when I woke up this morning, it's all pink, and I love it. Actually, that photograph is taken from the corner of my bed, so that's the view I wake up to every morning.

And even when I had no money, I mean, fortunately, I can afford to live in places like this now, but even when I had no money, I used to do the same thing. I would always, like I remembered being completely broke and being in France. I was living in a little town called Le Harve, up in the North.

I remember going around the whole town until I found the most beautiful street. And I remember thinking, "This is where I want to live," and I went and knocked on every single door in the street.

Halfway down the street, this guy opened the door and said, "Hey listen, you know what? I'm going to be in France for three months, do you have somewhere to rent? I'd love to live here."

And he said, "Why don't you come in a second." And he took me into the basement, and they just finished this brand new apartment and had another week of work to finish it. And there was this window that was 18 feet long and about 10 feet high that had the shutter on. You open up, and it was just this vista. And constantly I always say that's the choice. The choice is you don't have to have money to do that because it's everywhere—beauty is everywhere. And we just have to find and be conscious of it. Okay, I choose to do this. I choose to put my desk by this window because that one tree is beautiful, right?

▲**Deborah:** Oh, absolutely. I did not grow up with money for sure. I definitely was not in the wealthy category as I grew up and that was just part of my beautiful experience in itself. But what my Mom did and what she taught me was exactly what you're saying. She was so extraordinary and still is so extraordinary about being able to take what we have in the moment and transform it into a beautiful state and just aesthetically pleasing.

And she's always been able to do that and that really has formed within me even when I was nannying, and I lived literally in a converted garage for a family. And I had one room and a bathroom like that was it. And she just always helped me to see the beauty in that and that's the gift that I love, like you, to share that with other people because it's not as people say, "It's not about the money, it's about finding the beauty, it's about finding the gold, it's about making the choice to be happy right now and not waiting for X to happen."

Yeah, beautiful. David, thank you so much.

▲**David:** Well, thank you and we'll stay in touch. Remember, there's always a bed if you want to come and the guest room has a similar view. So if you're up here, and you want to come visit us, you're more than welcome.

▲**Deborah:** Absolutely.

So, thank you for that. I really appreciate it. And please let me know if there's anything that I can do for you, if something comes to mind that I can support you in some way, I'm here. So thank you so much.

▲**David:** Sounds great. Thank you lovely. I look forward to our blossoming friendship.

▲**Deborah:** I love it. I love it. Okay, blessings! Have a great day.

▲**David:** Bye!

I AM

Beth Hanishewski
Coach. Speaker. Spiritual Gangster.
www.mindsetcoaching.com

Beth is an international trainer, author and coach. She teaches people the art of relationship mastery with simple and powerful systems of life bliss and relationship transformation that deepens connections with people you love.

Beth specializes in helping women be happy(er). She is a highly intuitive coach with an uncanny ability to bring out the best in her clients and help them create lasting transformation in their lives. She began learning the path of a goddess, kicking and screaming, and was convinced that being a successful entrepreneur could only come with hard work, struggle and sacrifice.

It was only when she was completely exhausted and stressed out and her relationship was in shambles that she was open to learning a new way of doing things. Mastering simplicity and trusting her own femininity in a whole new way, she delights in sharing her findings and methods with others and is committed to helping woman become women of influence in a world that could use some goddess inspiration towards global change.

She shares her life with her husband, two children, two dogs and 10 chickens in Kelowna, BC Canada.

Deborah "Atianne" Wilson's Interview
with Beth Hanishewski

▲ **Deborah:** Good morning.

▲ **Beth:** How are you?

▲ **Deborah:** Good. I'm excited and decided to go ahead and press *Record*.

▲ **Beth:** I see that.

▲ **Deborah:** Well, because I get so excited. And who knows what could happen? We had this glorious conversation, and I'll get to the end and have a few tears because I forgot to key in the code to record.

▲ **Beth:** You'll go *oopsy-daisy*.

▲ **Deborah:** Okay. So, Beth—oh, my gosh—first of all, I'm so thankful. I see the word "glorious." It's like there's energy of just happiness and joy and sunshine to have a conversation with you. And I'm so thankful that you are so willing to be part of this experience, part of this co-creation of this book, because what I have found out in writing the book is that this is not as solitary as I once thought.

In fact, not a lot of it at all is solitary. In fact, just the idea of the intuitive qualities of what wants to come through and then the support that I've had from friends and family and colleagues, and I consider you all of that—friend, family, colleague all wrapped up in one. So, thank you so much for doing this. I really appreciate it.

▲ **Beth:** My pleasure.

▲ **Deborah:** Okay. So shall we begin officially (as if we haven't)? So, here's the deal. I was even revisiting the idea of your website, your current website as it stands today, and what strikes me is this title, this tagline, of "coach, speaker, happy girl" and the piece that quickly got related to what I talk about it in the book is celebration.

And I know that you and I have had many conversations, and more often than not, I can definitely say we start our conversations in a place of celebration—the "what's good," "what's up." I have chills as I even say that, so, to me, that is saying how important the idea of celebration is, and so I might go into two parts.

But I would love to share and hear your philosophy. How did you even tag yourself, own this phrase of *happy girl*, what brought you to this place, and why is celebration so important to you?

▲**Beth:** Two loaded, loaded questions.

▲**Deborah:** We're not about frivolous here. We're about going deep and going deep quick.

▲**Beth:** Yeah. No. Juicy. Okay. Well, I'll start with "happy girl," and I think that for me "happy girl" is a lifelong quest really to experience this place that I call happy, and I think over the years I would say that happy has been something I traditionally experienced when things are going well, right?

I've got love in my life. I've got money in my bank account. I'm feeling hot and sexy. I got all my girlfriends around me like a posse, and there I am happy, which as Marci Shimoff says in her book *Happy For No Reason*, it is like "if you can't be happy when everything is good, well, then, what does that say, right?" I think most people can be happy when everything is good. It's like going on vacation.

▲**Deborah:** Right.

▲**Beth:** If you can't be happy laying on a chaise lounge in the sun, in the tropics with some very hot waiter serving you a margarita, then there's a problem. So, for me being a happy girl, which is trying to find that place in myself where I feel happy, and happy is under the umbrella of what I call happy is lots of very high vibrational emotions—where I'm grateful, where I'm joyful, where I'm excited, where I'm inspired, where I'm just moved. Those to me are all emotions I equate with being happy. Even crying is being happy for me—when I'm releasing, and I'm just feeling everything so deeply. And, for me, this journey has been about trying to find that place in myself, *regardless* of my outside circumstances and sometimes in spite of my circumstances.

▲**Deborah:** Exactly.

▲**Beth:** Can I be happy when things are tough? Can I be happy when I'm not feeling well? Can I be happy when my business is struggling? Can I be happy when I'm really mad at my husband? That is really what my journey has been about. Am I happy, like awesome, every day? No, of course not.

But to me it's always a percentages game. I approach everything with moderation in the 80/20 rule. Am I happy most of the time? Yes. Is there certainly those days where I am really miserable and crabby? Absolutely. But I know *now* how to reach for happy. So, yeah, does that answer your question?

▲**Deborah:** Yeah, I love it. Well, yeah, it's just like the hub of the wheel that I can just spin off in all sorts of different directions, yes. And the words I use around feeling happy, feeling celebratory, is more often than not at the percentage scale that you are reaching for you, and you being the universal you, that more often than not we are feeling good, and being happy and being joyful and being healthy and all that comes with whatever we equate to our own spirituality our own wealth and, even more importantly, how do we get there, right? How do we, when we're not in that space, get there?

And so I'm wondering for you as a spiritual tool, how do you use celebration, especially like you touched on, which is so perfect and so in alignment with me. It touches on this idea like, okay, so when things aren't going so well, how do we be happy? How can we maybe celebrate those things maybe/maybe not in the moment but later? So, for you, personally, how is celebration a practice for you, if at all? And then, professionally, how does that weave into your own coaching style and your teaching from the stage about celebrating life?

▲**Beth:** Perfect. Well, celebration is a huge, huge part of my personal and professional life, and sometimes I don't think the line is quite blurry between those two.

▲**Deborah:** Absolutely. And, yes, it is.

▲**Beth:** So, therefore, my personal life affects my business every single day, which is why I think the art—if I call it—the art of celebration is so important. I was introduced to this actually from another coach way like early, early, early in my coaching practice days. I was really a newbie coach, and it was introduced to me as a way to always begin coaching conversation, and I sort of took that on, and I do it all the time. I find ways to celebrate in different ways in my life. So, I'll give you an example.

I have a girlfriend of mine who we don't see each other very much in our day-to-day lives, but we always, always meet on our birthdays for lunch. It is sort of this beautiful tradition we have, and we carve out this pocket of time, and we just break bread together. But it has become a tradition that when we meet because we haven't seen each other for a while, we always have to come of what we call the *birthday question* which is "what is the best thing that's happened to you this year?" and we share that always.

▲**Deborah:** What a great question!

▲**Beth:** Yeah, we share that on our birthdays. We always come with "What was the best thing that happened to you this year?" So, for us it's always about getting in and really digging into not just what was good and how you're doing which again is… you can… it's easy to stay in that superficial level—"Yeah, things are good. Kids are good. Dogs are good. Business is good," right? And then, anyway, then it's just a very light conversation, and then—saying, "what was the best thing that happened to you?"—it forces you to really sort of sift everything that happened and go, "Oh, this for me was the juiciest thing. This to me was my favorite thing and sometimes it's even a… it could be a painful thing."

▲**Deborah:** Sure. Absolutely.

▲**Beth:** But you reach for that as the best thing, right? So, that's one way I use celebration in my personal life. I use it with my family. We have another ritual we have called the P-I-N. So when we get together in a day, or I often do it when we're driving home from school or to activities, and of course I have incorporated all their friends. Anybody who is in the van has to play the PIN game.

And what you share is something positive, something interesting. And if you have, the only thing that's optional is the negative, it's the end. You don't have to share something negative, but if something happened to you that you're not happy about, that's the time you can share your negative.

But, because again you begin on celebration, you begin with what was good, you begin in what was interesting and then you may dive into what was not good. But again it sets this tone for celebration, and when I first started doing this with my daughter's gymnastic friends—I carpool along with this gaggle of gymnasts in my van, and I decided to do this PIN exercise, and my daughter is rolling her eyes in the back of her head like "my coach mother's coming out."

But now, this is like—fast-forward many years later. I'm still driving those same girls to the gym once a week. We all pile in my vehicle, and now they get in, and they fight to be the first to share.

▲**Deborah:** So cute.

▲**Beth:** And I love that, right? They're like "I'm going first, I'm going first. I got something," and it's like it's this beautiful ripple effect that's happening. This little tiny practice that I forced them into a few years ago has now become so normal, and if anybody new jumps in our carpool, the other girls are… they're the first to… "Hey. Just so you know you're going to have to say something positive before Beth drops you off like that's the rule." They just… it's beautiful.

▲**Deborah:** I love it.

▲**Beth:** So, that would be another way I use celebration. And in my coaching practice, it is mandatory. I have I think probably, like most coaches, I have a typical format that I follow with coaching. But maybe potentially what differentiates me from maybe other coaches is that I'm iron clad that my coaching sessions are sandwiched in celebration.

So, the very first thing that I ask my client to do is to celebrate something, and I do it very intentionally, and sometimes they don't want to. They whine and kick and scream, just like I did with my coach when I was told that I have to do that first, because if somebody gets on the phone, you're like "I just got to get in to like what's going on and what's challenging me and then what's hard."

But when you celebrate, it forces you again to get into that place of gratitude. It raises my vibration when I do that, and it raises their vibration. It raises everything about the call. And then from that place of what is good and what is working and what is beautiful in your life, then you can sort of put forth the challenge, and your mind is so much more able to be creative from a high-vibrational place than if we start with what's crap.

▲**Deborah:** Right. And even creative in the solutions is what I'm hearing — creative in the solutions, right?

▲**Beth:** Of course.

▲**Deborah:** I mean, that's really... that's the vibration I see that's so huge in this. It's like "Okay, if I can go here and when I can go here, then I'm opening up to something bigger, being able to come through rather than just kind of staying in that sticky sludge of the energy of the focus on the negative."

▲**Beth:** Exactly. So, that's my format. So, we'll go celebration then we create our contexts — the coachable, the challenge, that you want to dive into, right?

▲**Deborah:** Right.

▲**Beth:** We dive into that. We might do a process, or what have you. We come up with some action plan, and then we end on celebration. And so before, the last thing my client says before, we hang up is "What do you want to celebrate? What is your gem from this coaching session?"

And so we actually end on celebration as well. I shift "What was the best thing that happened to you this year?" into "What is the best part of this hour?" and I get to glean that gem before we close. So, I think celebration infuses every part of my life.

▲**Deborah:** I love it, I love it. And even from this place of celebration, like you had mentioned, and it is so easy to feel loving and feel joyful when people are in agreement with us, and we're feeling the same vibrational level and attitude level and mindset level and all that kind of stuff.

But when we're bumping into a challenge, a negative like in your PIN game with the kids, getting to the "oomph" of the problem that someone is bringing the challenge, the opportunity to a coaching session, I'm wondering... I want to weave in a conversation that we had a while ago when I was talking about having this wonderful stage, and I kept seeing this vision of a place I take my coaching clients to—even on my radio show—it's like "Okay. So this is the place you're at, right? It's that sludgy place. It's that feeling uncomfortable place. It's something's that triggered them."

And I just want to have two screens, and I talked about this in the book. It's like I had these two screens, and they were like, "Now what? So, now what are you going to do?" And a gem that you gave me that is so worthy of celebration is you're like "Well, why don't you just change one of those to 'So What!'" And what I love about that is it was so perfect for me and my style of coaching with lots of love, that kind of angelic kick-butt coaching style like "Okay. So what? You are where you are, and now from here we're going to do what? Now, what are you going to do with it?"

So, from that place of that conversation—if you remember that, which was so great—in what I call "Finding the Gold," even in the PIN game with your kids, they presented something negative about where they are in that moment. What is maybe a kind of a big-ticket item is what I'm hearing way that you help to reframe people to find that nugget because it's that nugget that we can also celebrate, right?

▲**Beth:** Yeah, totally. So, yeah. And again everything comes from my own struggles, my own time in the pit, so to speak, right?

▲**Deborah:** Absolutely, of course.

▲**Beth:** In that quicksand, that quagmire, where they just cannot see how this could be possibly good. To me, it always comes back to the questions that you ask and so that's why you said, "Well, I'm in the situation and that's where that 'So What?' comes in. So what?" But it's not *so what* like, "Who cares?" It's "So What?"

▲**Deborah:** No, of course not.

▲**Beth:** So what are you going to do about it is basically where that question goes because what I find is that it's easy—and I'll just try to talk in the first person. It's easy to say third person, but I'll just talk first person. I think that's more powerful. That when I'm in a situation that I'm really unhappy about, it's easy for me to get caught up in the "Why?" – "Why is this happening? Why is my husband doing that? Why isn't this easier for me?" Why blah-blah-blah?—and I can go down a rabbit hole, and that what sends me down the rabbit hole is asking, "Why this is happening?"

▲**Deborah:** Absolutely.

▲**Beth:** And the truth is the "Why?" is really what I consider the lowest-quality question you can ask yourself because the truth is we either (a) we'll never know why, or (b) it doesn't really matter even if we did. So, if you look at something extreme like "Why are there so many children starving in the world?" Well, what does it matter why? It's much more important and much better and more effective to ask, "What do we want to do about that?"

▲**Deborah:** Right. It's more empowering.

▲**Beth:** Who cares? It doesn't matter why, especially "So what?" So what that whatever contributed to the demise of the current situation? I mean, yes, you can create from understanding. Definitely, there are some things you can put in for context or what can we learn for next time.

But, generally speaking, what I like to ask is a question that takes me out of the past of reflection, which is what "Why?" does and wonder why that happened and move me into the now or the future—where do I want to go from here? So, I always say, if you find yourself in this funk, ask yourself the highest-quality questions you can, and they would be questions like "What do I want to do?" and "How can I use this?" and "Where could this lead me next?" Those to me are 10,000 times more powerful questions than a why will ever get me.

▲**Deborah:** Absolutely. And, oh my God, an *amen* to that one. And, literally, I just had a conversation like two days ago with a client who I am attempting—right? Because she can only receive what she's open to receive—but steering her in the direction of just what you said. Her idea is wanting to process like "I need to know," and this is a very egoic piece, and I want to hear your thoughts on that very egoic piece too, which is very low vibration to want to know the why of how she is the way she is today and why she gets triggered in certain things.

And my question to her that day was "What if you never understand why? What if you never know why? What will you do?" Right? It's that "Now what?" What will you do then?" And that is often very shocking because the ego is a very sabotaging piece of energy in that moment of saying, "if we just know why, then it's all going to be good," and it really delays, I think, our inner growth on so many levels. What's your thought?

▲**Beth:** I think you're absolutely 100% right, that you might as well just... it's like your thought pushing the brakes right there and then. It's like taking a detour, pulling your car over and getting out. You're not traveling at all when you stopped to do that, in that place of inquiry, "Why?"

When I want to use a metaphor, I think of the most extreme one I can think of which to me is death, right? Think of all the people who have died in the world without saying goodbye, without leaving a note, without telling everybody what their wishes were, without resolving an argument, without paying off their debt, whatever. And they leave people in the space "Why? Why did you die? Why did you leave? Why didn't you do this before you left this earth?" Right?

▲**Deborah:** Right.

▲**Beth:** And that question you'll never know because they're not here to give you the answer, and people get really caught up on this "I need closure. I needed them to just tell me why, so I can move on," and I just think that is such bullshit. That is not necessary to move on.

▲**Deborah:** True.

▲**Beth:** You don't need to know why. Again, you just need to know what or how can you use it.

▲**Deborah:** Right. How can you use it? This how-can-you-use-it is... so, for me it's "Finding the Gold." And, again, we all teach from the place of what we have experienced, what we've learned and what works for us, right?

And so this flavor of *Finding the Gold*, finding the nugget, I'm like "Forget the 'silver lining,' let's go higher than that." I don't need a lining—although I love the movie—but I want the gold. I want to extract the most delicious nugget I can because for me it's the way I personally cleaned up my own health. I cleaned up my own finances, I cleaned up... you name it.

It just got better. It became better than what it was and continues to get better. It doesn't mean it's perfect in some fantasy-perfect world, but it's better and better. And, so, for me *Finding the Gold* is super, super, super—did I say super?—important. So, what is the language you use for it? Is it nugget? I just would love to know your language on it because we all have a different language for the exact same thing.

▲**Beth:** Yes, I like nugget a lot. I think I use gem.

▲**Deborah:** Gem, yeah. See? But it's all got this royal quality. It's got treasure quality, right?

▲**Beth:** Kind of a sparkling thing. I think one of the reasons I use gem is I identify with the concept of alchemy, and to me this idea of transformation, which is really overused in the personal development world, but I think that everybody is offering a transformation of some sort.

▲**Deborah:** Right.

▲**Beth:** But I think that at the heart of the word *transformation* is to me alchemy. This idea of taking something—so, like, in the natural world, it's like taking coal, and it becoming a diamond, taking... and it becoming gold, right? You like to use gold a lot, right?

▲**Deborah:** Right.

▲**Beth:** That to me is alchemy, and that's probably why I use that word.

▲**Deborah:** I love it. It's high vibration for sure. I love it.

▲**Beth:** To me, it's about taking that grit, taking that sludge, taking that what is not so attractive or often I use the gift that is wrapped in a really brown, stinky paper bag, right? We all want presents with beautiful bows and that are eloquent and so pretty you can't wait to break it open.

▲**Deborah:** Right.

▲**Beth:** But the truth is most of the best gifts that we only usually appreciate in hindsight are the paper-bag-wrapped ones. That's where we grow. Those are our invitations to really lean in to what is going on. Otherwise, it's like that how do you sharpen a saw, right? You need friction. How do pearls get made with grit, with sand?

▲**Deborah:** Right.

▲**Beth:** That to me—I use those sort of metaphors—when you have grit in your life, how can you turn that into a pearl?

▲**Deborah:** Right. I love that.

▲**Beth:** But to me, it's really about alchemy because the alchemy is really about changing the belief you have about a situation. So, can you shift your belief? So, for example, let's say you had a friend who un-friends you. I've gone through this and it was, and I think, harder than a boyfriend break-up. I was so traumatized by being un-friended by this person who I just loved so much, and so I could have told myself a big story.

So it was big, big, big grit in my life, and I was in pain about it. And I did ask myself, "Why, why, why? Why, why, why? Why won't she talk? Why can't we repair this? Why... can't I do anything about this? Why did this happen?" Again, it's not useful, not helpful, and it just kept me stuck in that place of feeling sad and hurt and gross and really in shame.

I was embarrassed like I was un-friended, like I must be pretty bad, and it triggered every crappy thing I'd ever thought about myself—about being unworthy, about being unlovable, about abandonment—you name it. I got triggered by this event. This seemingly small event sent me on this huge exploration of what does this mean.

And so for me, I had to shift the belief because I was making it about her and what she had done and how this whole scene had played out, and in the end I just had to go, "I don't know why this happened." So it took me awhile—even though I teach it—it took me a long time to go "So what?" You don't know why it happened, it just did.

And in that place where I could challenge the belief, does that mean I'm unlovable? No. Does it mean I'm unworthy? No. Does it mean I'm a bad person? No. Can something be learned from this situation? Oh, yes. Much could be learned from that situation. Can I grow? Can I do better? Oh, yes. Could I have handled things differently? Yes. What will I do next time? Ahh...this is what I would do.

And so that is an example of how I take that and I alchemized it so that it no longer has that charge on me, it no longer has that hold on me. Do I still feel sad when I think of this friend that used to be in my life? Sure. But it doesn't, like, rack me like I can't function. It doesn't have that hold on me anymore.

▲**Deborah:** I love that. Holy Cow! It's huge, Beth, and we're not talking about "Facebook un-friending" because often when we hear the word un-friending now with the whole Facebook thing, it's like someone you... yeah, they just decided not to like you anymore and they just yeah... But even that, as simple as that seems, can in comparison to a deep, harmonious friendship at one time, someone you might even call your sister, even the trigger of being *Facebook unfriended* is big for people. People freak out, right?

▲**Beth:** Absolutely, because, again, it is those old wounds that you're unlovable, right?

▲**Deborah:** Absolutely.

▲**Beth:** And we hear that all the time. This person is blocking me. This person... I don't get to see their feed, and it's crazy that we live in a social media world where that has become important.

▲**Deborah:** Right.

▲**Beth:** Who do you have access to? It's really interesting what Facebook has done, and just like any great technology, it has that Divine side, and it has a diabolical side, right?

▲**Deborah:** Right, the light and the dark.

▲**Beth:** Yeah. We have cyber bullying because of Facebook, and we have people who are getting kidneys donated because of Facebook.

▲**Deborah:** Yes. It's extraordinary. Well, and it shows the full spectrum as does the opportunity of really any situation—just the full spectrum. To me it's just not the black and white, and it's not even the gray. I've changed gray to this idea of full spectrum, like there's just such a full spectrum of light in-between, I see situations in color, and it's kind of like spinning the wheel, like spinning the roulette wheel or something, like you can land anywhere and that's a choice, and it just depends on where you'd like to go and how far you can go with it. It's amazing.

Beth, in regard to many of the clients you reach, and I know you work with a lot of women *and* men where some people are very, you know, they just attract one over the other. I want to talk about some energy, your philosophy, your wisdom around the ability to receive, and healing those parts of us—because you were just talking about the wound, right?—about a lot of the wounds that often many of us carry: abandonment, low self-esteem, the unworthiness piece, all those things where—the "not enoughness," I often call it—just this chronic *not enoughness* where perfectionism comes in and all sorts of other hairy things.

So, this idea of—and it's more maybe not even posed as a particular question but just as an opening to being able to receive the many ways that I feel—Spirit, God, whatever words people would like to pop in here—that we are gifted these reminders of our worthiness and how often—I know for me because I do work with a lot of women—often people are unable to receive and, therefore, to me, keep that wound open.

So, I wonder if you would just speak with your philosophy about being able to receive in all its forms and really heal in that wound of unworthiness. Another big one. Nothing small here, Beth, you know that.

▲Beth: How long do we have?

▲Deborah: Well, we have enough time to definitely touch on, to go to some high points, low points, in-between, full-spectrum points. You know that's the beauty of this.

▲Beth: You know, this idea of receiving. I think it is, it is at the heart, certainly it's the heart of me, I think, and also the heart of my coaching practice, particularly coaching women, but men, as well, but I think women definitely have cornered the market on this inability to be good receivers, and we could look at all kinds of ways that it's been culturally cultivated and historically cultivated that women are the givers—we are the caretakers, we are the nurturers, and so we have a long history, long-standing habit of being givers.

So, I think giving becomes natural to women in particularly--not to say it doesn't to men, but I think particularly women have acute sensitivity to what people need, and they often will just pour it into other people. The problem with only doing this beautiful love expression one way is like any other thing. Eventually, it's like that bucket runs out where you don't have anything to give because you haven't learned to replenish, and I think that the number-one place to build your receiving muscle is with yourself, which we often think of receiving as something you get from another person, like if somebody buys you a present or sends you for a massage, or buys you a coffee, and you can receive that.

But I think that the place to build your muscle around receiving is through the practice of exceptional self-care, where you, yourself, recognize, "Oh, I'm feeling depleted," "Oh, I'm feeling tired," "Ooh, I'm feeling like I'm starting to resent the people I'm giving to all the time." Yikes! To me, those are all clues that you need some self-care, that you need some restoration.

And for every woman, it's something different, and, for me, I have a whole list of things that help me to restore and replenish the tank, that proverbial tank that we talk about, and I think that is the place to begin this idea of healing because when you can give to yourself—and here's the kicker—where you can receive something, do something nice for yourself whether it's a bubble bath or a weekend away or something even more extravagant — and *do so guilt-free.*

▲**Deborah:** The *kicker.* Ha, ha.

▲**Beth:** That is the kicker. That is the caveat. You must be able to do this. Because actually we'll say, "Oh, I went away, but I felt guilty the whole time." It's like "I ate a chocolate cake, but I hated myself." Well, then, that's not acts of receiving. That's just being practicing being self-abusive, it's self-abusive. If you're going to eat the cake, be like Julia Child, enjoy every bite. Right?

If you go to the spa, drink it in. Somebody else is rubbing your feet like just... think about the luxury of that beautiful act of receiving. So, anyway, I think that there is so much, many nuances, but, when a woman is good at taking care of herself, I feel it makes — positions you — to be a good receiver for other people, and what people forget, and this is probably what I coach women on a lot, is that giving feels good, and so this is how sometimes I help women get over receiving.

As I said, you know how good you feel when you've done something kind or thoughtful or generous to somebody else? And they're like, "Yeah, that's awesome." I said give that feeling, give the gift of that feeling, to someone else.

▲**Deborah:** Absolutely.

▲**Beth:** That's what you do when you receive. You say, "You get to be the good person. You get to be the good guy here."

▲**Deborah:** The hero, right? The heroine.

▲**Beth:** You get to be the heroine or the hero. You get to be the giver, and I'll be a receiver today and let you experience the joy of giving, and then we'll switch, and then I'll experience the joy of receiving and then we'll switch back again, and that to me creates a flow of energy, so when you look at how... the people who like, who talk about Chi and all these beautiful ways that you can create abundance and love in your life is always around energies. Where is your stuck energy?

But, to me, if you want to be very successful, if you want to be very happy, if you want to be very attractive to opportunities and people and situations, you must — that flow — must be able to come in and out just like a door. So, to me, when you build your receiving muscle, you build the flow of energy in and out from you to the world, and I think that's why it's so important. So, when I assign people these practices of self-care they're like "How many bubble baths do I have to take?" It's not about the bubble bath. It's really about building the hinges of that door to swing both ways so that all things can come in and out that you want in your life.

▲**Deborah:** I love it. I love it. Yeah. Oh my gosh. It's so perfect. I'm laughing about the bubble bath piece because as I think many coaches, especially people who coach women at this idea of self-care in the form of a bubble bath just seems so trivial to people. I was just coaching a woman who wants to have a child. She has not had a child, yet, and that is to her a huge essence of who she was meant to be. She's meant to be a mother.

And, so, we were talking about the "Why?" and that's actually shocking. You would think people could quickly answer why would you want to be a mother and she needed to really self-reflect so we worked on that and then what came to me intuitively was "Well, what are the qualities you want to expand here, the energetic qualities?" And one of the things that came she's like "to be caring, to be loving," and so then we really brought it back to her: "How can you be more loving to you? How can you bring more self-care to you?"

And I didn't tell her the reason, the ways, if you will. I had her go inside. So, "What can you imagine that would be for you?" and that was hysterical. We kind of giggled about it of course after, but I knew how important it was in that one of her images of being loving to herself, she saw herself in a bubble bath. I hadn't mentioned it ever in our coaching, and she instantly pushed that aside, and I think this is what we can often do with our own intuitive hits, is we push them aside because we judge them too quickly as not being important.

And as simplistic as a bubble bath may sound to many people, people who read this book, those often simplistic things are the very answer you need to receive that next step. Wouldn't you agree?

▲**Beth:** Absolutely. I think it is the easiest place to start: (a) it's free; (b) you don't have to go outside, you don't have to travel.

▲**Deborah:** Right.

▲**Beth:** You just need to carve out the time.

▲**Deborah:** Right. Absolutely. And I told her, "What time do you need?" I'm like –

▲**Beth:** And it's like that with chocolate cake. Give yourself the gift to absolutely enjoy it, whether you sit in a bath for five minutes or five hours. But give yourself a gift of truly, truly soaking up that luxury, that place where you're like, "Yes. I'm worth pampering."

▲**Deborah:** Right. And giving up that idea of doing and just *being* and how the quality of being is so inherent in our overall happiness for sure. Love it. You touched on something in self-care just a moment ago about clients, people, us as individuals as well being aware when our tank is low, if you will. I'm not sure what words you use, but that idea of not coming from a full place and how coming from a full place we can really, really give.

I'd love for you to just speak to the idea of our bodies getting our attention, our bodies helping us to understand where we are and supporting our overall good, even when we get sick, even when we get injured. Just coming back to this idea of how that can be, I mean I wouldn't celebrate "Gee, I'm so happy that I have a broken leg" or something—but the idea of the gift that that can give us to maybe slow down or whatever. So, I'd love to have you speak to that—this idea that our body is giving us clues to where we are on our journey.

▲**Beth:** Yeah, absolutely. I think probably Christine Northrup was the first author that I ever read on *Women's Bodies, Women's Wisdom* that really sort of introduced me to the concept of this idea that there is a connection between mind and body and our emotional well-being and our physical well-being. And over the years, I have read so many teachers and authors and beautiful minds that really reinforce this idea that wellness comes from within, and when we're not well, it's an invitation for us to look at what is going on in our lives.

So, I think that like we've said, any time that you experience even tension, even a headache, all the way to a full-blown serious illness, it's an invitation to look at not so much, again, not the "why, why is this happening," but "what could this be illuminating for me right now?" And I always choose—I have this practice, this habit… every year I choose a word of the year, and I let that word kind of be my North Star. It sort of guides my year.

And so, two years ago, my word of the year was *simplicity,* and I just got so, I got a warm fuzzy feeling, and I got chills and I thought of simplicity and my life just being simple because I was feeling really not simple the year before, really overwhelmed by many things.

So I thought, "Okay, this will be the year of simplicity" and it's like I claimed the word and immediately forgot it the next moment, because I decided in January to launch all kinds of things in my business. I was speaking, I was doing workshops, I was doing live events, I was just going crazy. Instead of making my life simpler, I actually ramped it up. I don't know if I could have done any more. I was going flat out.

I basically went flat out until May, and I was noticing I was feeling tired. But of course like many overachievers that override, the first clue that you should maybe give your body some attention. I was busy. I'm like "Okay, once I'm done in my event, once I'm done with _____, I'll rest."

So, sure enough, I pushed all the way through, through my live weekend intensive and I then thought "Okay, I had the whole next week off," and I booked massage, I booked some reiki. I was in my mind doing everything right to replenish the old tank.

The thing I didn't count on was that my tank wasn't just, like, kind of empty. It was totally empty with absolutely nothing left and after a few days when I noticed I totally was not feeling better. I felt so tired. I was like I want to go to sleep after lunch and like, "I just need a little nap." I was falling asleep at 8 o'clock at night, and it was then that I was diagnosed with being anemic, but, like, really, really anemic like the kind of anemia where my iron is too low.

The doctors phone me and said like "If it goes lower," like, "we're going to have to hospitalize you," like, "you have nothing in your body in terms of iron reserve." I'm like "oh that explains why I'm kind of tired." They're like "kind of tired, how do you function?" and I'm like "yeah."

And so that whole thing once I realized how tired I was and how depleted I was and of course I had all these other things I'm planning on launching for the summer, post my event, and I really got that the gift of anemia—and it really was a gift to me—because I went if my body is shutting down like this, it is clearly trying to send me a message, and it was in that moment where I was laying there feeling so tired, I remembered my word of the year, that I had sort of forgotten...

▲Deborah: The one you tucked away.

▲Beth: Yeah. Sort of like a ball of paper in the corner that I've thrown in January, and I sort of picked that word back up, and I thought, "How can I simplify things for me now so that I can rest?"

And I took everything extra off my plate. I canceled all my things I was planning to launch in that fall, in that summer and the fall, and I just cocooned.

And I just maintained my private practice, a little bit of business, and I really just rested. I basically did almost as little as I possibly could get away with doing all summer long, and it was such a gift to me. And I think that when we lean into illness of any kind, and you can find "Okay, how can I use this?" Some people I think get sick in order to learn how to receive and ask for help.

▲**Deborah:** Absolutely.

▲**Beth:** That's a gift for them because they get sick, and they got to realize they can't do it all themselves, and they kind of put it out there like "can somebody help me?" and they're overwhelmed. I can't tell you how many women are phoning and weeping. They go "I cannot believe how many people are doing these nice things for you."

▲**Deborah:** Right.

▲**Beth:** And that becomes the gift. It's the illness, per se, that's the gift, but it's the other things—sometimes even a headache. If I get a headache especially if it's right at my temples, I will often ask myself this question. I'm like "What is it that I can't see?" Because I feel like it's right in my vision, my headache.

▲**Deborah:** Right.

▲**Beth:** And I'll just kind of wait for that intuitive answer. I know you would love that.

▲**Deborah:** Of course.

▲**Beth:** So, what is it that I can't see, and I'll just sort of put it out there and see what I get.

▲**Deborah:** Absolutely.

▲**Beth:** So I think that our bodies always give us clues whether they're tiny little tensions and, or, like I said, full-blown illnesses. We are always given clues to the extent that we pay attention, I think is our... to the extent that we experience full-blown illnesses.

▲**Deborah:** Oh, yes. I can attest to that as you know. Oh my gosh, well said. Oh my gosh. Perfect. All of it perfect. I really love and enjoy everything that you said. Oh, my gosh. I know all of it seems so serious. I'm sure we'll love it when it's being read on paper. Definitely what we will be missing is your beautiful voice, the tone, and the fun that comes with your voice, but I'm just going to trust that it's all going to come through with the words there because I know...

▲**Beth:** Maybe ask me a silly question.

▲**Deborah:** Yeah. Do you believe in the Easter bunny?

▲**Beth:** I believe in everything.

▲**Deborah:** I don't know why that came up. I am all about—you know me, I'm "Christmas Excited"—I'm like, "forget the one day, let's go for it all – birthday excited, Christmas Excited, Hanukkah, Kwanzaa, I don't care. Find something and let's get excited about it for sure." Oh my gosh, well what a blessing. I could talk to you all day. Let's just yammer and roll with it and celebrate and go into it all.

And I love that you're so willing to just go so deep, and I love that you are not about the superficiality about it and just truly promoting well-being on all levels and freedom of the soul. I just really see that in you, and I thank you for that.

▲**Beth:** Thank you.

▲**Deborah:** You're welcome.

▲**Beth:** I feel like I should be lighter. I should end on lightness.

▲**Deborah:** Insert…what did you say?

▲**Beth:** I said like I should end on some lightness. Oh, you know what? I will end on lightness, if you have one more minute.

▲**Deborah:** It was all Light by the way. It's all perspective. It was all Light, but go ahead.

▲**Beth:** Sometimes I can be terribly morose. You're right.

▲**Deborah:** No. Not at all.

▲**Beth:** A girlfriend of mine that I worked together with—the same girlfriend, by the way, that I do the birthday question with—years ago, we ran an event company together, and we called ourselves the Fun Team, and we always had matching outfits, and we showed up in all these events, and that was part of our branding that if you saw us in matching outfits, we were clearly doing an event, and it was loads and loads and loads of fun.

I mean, just planning the outfits was fun let alone just working together and then that kind of marketing that we were up to. But we had a motto that was actually on our business cards, and some people were really surprised by this, but our motto on our business card was "If it isn't fun, what's the point?" and I still, I live by that mantra all the time because I think if you want to bring lightness and joy into your life, you must align yourself with a mantra like that.

▲**Deborah:** Right.

▲**Beth:** And some people think, "Well, I know everything can be fun." Well, actually quite a bit. I don't know. I can even make toilet cleaning fun if I try. Almost everything can be joyful. Sometimes you just need to add the spice of that, right? Sometimes you need to add wines, you need to add chocolate, sometimes you need to have friends, sometimes you had to have music—you can always add something to make it fun.

▲But I make decisions in my life. I have all kinds of criteria for how I say yes and no to different requests that are made for me, and I can have shining objects syndrome. I can have lots of opportunities. I can "Oh, I should do that. Oh, I should do this" but in the end, sometimes it will come down to that question "Would this be fun for me?"

▲**Deborah:** Great.

▲**Beth:** And if that is a yes, I'm pretty much ready to go. And it's very much— and this is what brings us back to you when you asked me and said "could I interview you and just sort of get your take on a few things?" and to me if someone said "well, would that be fun for me?" It's pure joy for me. It's pure joy for me for you to have me be a part of this. It's a pure joy for me to go into these topics and deep dive if we want to or shallow it if we choose and just not have an agenda or other than just to have fun—have fun with all of these topics that affect every one of us. So, I think that's what I would end on, "if it isn't fun, what's the point?"

▲**Deborah:** I agree, absolutely, because we often get trapped in that have-to, and then we can always shift our mindset around that and go "What do we get to do? What are we choosing to do?" and I love it, and I love you, Beth, and you got me all teary-eyed. And considering that this is joyful and fun to delve in these arenas and these energies and these areas that we compartmentalize, but yet all of it affects the overall quality of our life, and it is about the quality because in truth if you're not feeling joyful and happy about it, what is the point? I love it, and I love you and I'm so thankful. Thank you, sweetie.

▲**Beth:** Thank you. Have a fun day.

▲**Deborah:** Heck, yeah. I love it. Okay, beautiful. I will talk to you soon and blessings to you, your family, and your overall joy in life. How's that?

▲**Beth:** It's fun. Thank you, darling. Au revoir.

▲**Deborah:** Bye-bye.

Share the Love!

Tell me how this book is positively making a difference for you. I would love to hear what is creating a change within you and touching your heart from connecting in with my passionate work.

I invite you to share your letters or e-mail messages with me:

Deborah "Atianne" Wilson
Angels And Prosperity
PO Box 7119
Boulder, CO 80306

Deborah@angelsandprosperity.com

Feel the Love

Please visit my websites to see my latest offerings and programs and learn how I can support you to create a life of freedom.

www.angelsandprosperity.com
www.onenessbecomesyou.com

Booking Deborah & Quantity Discounts

Interested in booking Deborah for your event or program?

Quantity discounts for her books, home-study course or Oneness Becomes You™ music are available.

Contact our office at
774-31A-NGEL

Made in the USA
San Bernardino, CA
16 February 2014